SACRED JOURNEY TO ATLANTIS

by

DR. NORMA J. MILANOVICH

and

JEAN MELTESEN

 ATHENA Publishing

First Edition, 1992

ISBN 0-9627417-3-6

Library of Congress Catalog Card Number 92-71209

Cover Illustration: David Gittens

Cover Design: Robert K. Mortensen

**Published by
ATHENA PUBLISHING
Mossman Center, Suite 206
7410 Montgomery Blvd. NE
Albuquerque, NM 87109-1574
FAX (505) 880-1623**

Printed in the United States of America
10 9 8 7 6 5 4 3 2 1

Come to the edge, he said.

They said: We are afraid.

Come to the edge, he said.

They came.

He pushed....and they flew.

Guillaume Apollinaire

SACRED JOURNEY TO ATLANTIS

DEDICATION

THIS BOOK is dedicated to the 144,000 Starseeds who have journeyed to Earth to reclaim their power and serve in the Light of Our Most Radiant One. These Starseeds are of the highest vibrations and are destined to surpass all previous expectations deemed possible by third or fourth dimensional Beings. As humans are transformed into the Fifth Kingdom and Dimension, these way-showers will lead the masses to greater truths and establish the kingdom of Light and love which will testify to the oneness of God. Their journeys will unmask the ancient wisdom of Atlantis, and will encompass the unveiling of the mysteries that have been hidden for over 10,000 years.

(Dedication transmitted by Ascended Master Kuthumi)

THE APOCALYPSE

APOCALYPSE IMPLIES revelation. It means a vision of things that were, are, and are yet to come.

Some have written that St. John, the apostle (who is recorded to have been Ascended Master Kuthumi in a former embodiment), was directed by the Office of the Christ to record the vision that Christ is the One who is destined to return to Earth. He was guided to instruct the elders of the seven churches of Asia Minor of this occurrence and to record his visions of what was and is yet to come. The messages in THE APOCALYPSE provide hope, with a clear understanding that victory will only be attained with a struggle.

Two of the passages from THE APOCALYPSE are especially interesting as they speak of the 144,000. Since Masters Kuthumi, El Morya, and Delphor dedicated the book to this group, we feel these passages are of interest to the reader.

Chapter 7 of the Apocalypse

The Number That Were Marked with the Seal of the Living God.

> After this I saw four angels standing at the four corners of the Earth, holding fast the four winds of the Earth, that no wind should blow over the

Earth, or over the sea, or upon any tree. 2 And I saw another angel ascending from the rising of the sun, having the seal of the living God; and he cried with a loud voice to the four angels, who had it in their power to harm the Earth and the sea, 3 saying, "Do not harm the Earth or the sea or the trees, till we have sealed the servants of our God on their foreheads." 4 And I heard the number of those who were sealed, a hundred and forty-four thousand sealed, out of every tribe of the children of Israel; 5 of the tribe of Judah, twelve thousand sealed; of the tribe of Ruben, twelve thousand; of the tribe of Gad, twelve thousand; 6 of the tribe of Aser, twelve thousand; of the tribe of Nephthali, twelve thousand; of the tribe of Manasses, twelve thousand; 7 of the tribe of Simeon, twelve thousand; of the tribe of Levi, twelve thousand; of the tribe of Issachar, twelve thousand; 8 of the tribe of Zebulon, twelve thousand; of the tribe of Joseph, twelve thousand; of the tribe of Benjamin, twelve thousand sealed.

9 After this I saw a great multitude which no man could number, out of all nations and tribes and peoples and tongues, standing before the throne and before the Lamb, clothed in white robes, and with palms in their hands. 10 And they cried with a loud voice, saying, "Salvation belongs to our God who sits upon the throne, and to the Lamb." 11 And all the angels were standing round about the throne, and the elders and the four living creatures; and they fell on their faces before the throne and worshipped God, 12 saying, "Amen. Blessing and glory and wisdom and thanksgiving and honor and power and strength to our God forever and ever. Amen."

13 And one of the elders spoke and said to me, "These who are clothed in white robes, who are they? and whence have they come?" 14 And I said to him, "My lord, thou knowest." And He said to me, "These are they who have come out of the great tribulation, and have washed their robes and made them white in the blood of the Lamb. 15 Therefore they are before the throne of God, and serve Him day and night in His temple, and He who sits upon the throne will dwell with them. 16 They shall neither hunger nor thirst anymore, neither shall the sun strike them nor any heat. 17 For the Lamb who is in the midst of the throne will shepherd them, and will guide them to the fountains of the waters of life, and God will wipe away every tear from their eyes."

Chapter 14 of the Apocalypse

The Lamb and the Virgins Who Follow Him.

And I saw, and behold, the Lamb was standing upon Mount Sion, and with Him a hundred and forty-four thousand having His name and the name of His Father written on their foreheads. 2 And I heard a voice from heaven like a voice of many waters, and like a voice of loud thunder; and the voice that I heard was as of harpers playing on their harps. 3 And they were singing as it were a new song before the throne, and before the four living creatures and the elders; and no one could learn the song except those hundred and forty-four thousand, who have been purchased from the Earth. 4 These are they who were not defiled with women; for they are virgins. These follow the Lamb wherever He goes. These were purchased from among men, first-fruits unto God and unto the Lamb, 5 and in their mouth there was found no lie; they are without blemish.

Because of concerns regarding specific wording of this latter passage, the following question was addressed to Master Kuthumi; his reply also follows.

KUTHUMI, THIS PASSAGE IMPLIES THAT ONLY MEN ARE ENTITLED TO BE OF THE GROUP CALLED THE 144,000. IT ALSO APPEARS TO CONTAIN A DEROGATORY STATEMENT REGARDING WOMEN. WOULD YOU EXPLAIN THIS PASSAGE AND TELL US IF THIS IS TRULY WHAT IS MEANT?

Dearest Daughters in the Light of the Most Radiant One. I thank you for this opportunity to explain the words and the energy that accompanies those words, for in the decoding of this message is revealed one of the secrets of the Kingdom. I come as your guide today, and in this role, I will guide you to another awareness that is destined to shed a different perspective on the preconceived notions that could be formed when interpreting that passage from a literal viewpoint.

The times in which these words were recorded reflected the nature of the minds of the people in embodiment and, consequently, the conditions of the society created from the thoughts that prevailed. Centuries ago, the paradigms that were current demanded that only those in male embodiment be allowed to pursue positions of power, government, instruction, and wealth. Therefore, only the souls who were of male gender were allowed to make their marks in the annals of history without paying a high price to the society in which they resided.

This mindset meant that females had limited opportunities to practice certain rituals or take stands, especially those of a political nature. The men of the societies were allowed to express their opinions and to practice their belief systems in the physical world. This does not mean that the females could not do so, but they certainly were restricted in so doing, for they often feared for their lives and their positions in society. Therefore, few in female embodiment took stands or had opportunities to act out their belief systems. For those who did, their contributions and courage were seldom recorded in the annals of your history textbooks.

As a result, in order to act out a commitment to a belief system and to be tested as an initiate on the path to God, one had to choose to incarnate in male embodiment to have the opportunity to prove that the courage to take a stand actually matched that belief system. Is that not truly the test for a value system?

The passage you have recorded for this document actually implies that the 144,000 souls, who today stand around the Lamb, were once in male embodiment and took a stand for their spiritual beliefs. They died for their belief systems in a former lifetime. They did even more than that. In that previous lifetime, they also devoted their entire life to God and to serving their own Christ Self in the name of God. In taking the vows of poverty and chastity, they turned from the temptation of forming a union with a female in embodiment, in order that they might devote their entire will to know and serve God.

The wording in the passage is not intended to mean that the female energy is of lesser quality. Instead, it is meant to mean that the focus of the souls in their male embodiments was not divided in that lifetime. They actually learned to develop their own feminine energies within their consciousness. Rather than turning to the outside for their answers, and learning that that journey is futile, they dedicated their training program to understanding the inner paths of Light and love.

The passage implies just that, although the true words and original meaning have been slightly altered by human hands during the course of the centuries. That is why it appears to be slightly distorted in its resonance today.

Look at the interpretation now from the perspective of the times and from the viewpoint of the yin and yang energy. Know that each soul in embodiment is a combination of both, and that in the refinement on the path to mastery, a soul must incarnate as both male and female to perfect the qualities of both. A soul cannot survive with only half the supply of energy, either male or female. This is truth. In order to become one with the God Force, each soul must balance these energies within the mind and heart connection. One perfect way to accomplish this is to live as both male and female, in different lifetimes.

So, Dear Ones, know that gender in this lifetime does not preclude any soul from being among the group to sit around the Lamb. In the passage it referred to the gender in which the first ascension was accomplished. In reality there are many more souls than 144,000 that presently grace His path and show the way. The group marked by God in that passage are those who will be the way-showers in the future to teach others of truths they learned in accomplishing tests and initiations that led to the understanding of higher truths and consciousness.

The number one hundred and forty-four adds up to nine. Nine is the number of completion. This means that this group, when their work and instruction is complete, will be taken from the Earth to journey to higher kingdoms of consciousness, after their present incarnations are done. Their work will be completed when they bring in the truths that will set humans free. They work for the Father/ Mother of the oneness of the All to shed Light and love on the beloved Terra.

I thank you for asking me to interpret this passage. I AM Kuthumi, your informant for this interpretation of love. I hope this answer serves to shed a new perspective on the interpretation, as promised in the opening remarks. Adonai.

ACKNOWLEDGMENTS

WE THANK Masters Kuthumi, El Morya, Delphor, and the other great ones who so patiently and lovingly guide our journey, that we may receive illumination. These radiant Masters walk beside us and honor our choices no matter how difficult our paths. Their support and love are unending.

Had it not been for their encouragement and assistance, we would never have made this sacred journey to Atlantis. Through their instruction we have learned that Atlantis is not only real, but is also alive in the heart of any soul who wishes to discover it.

We thank Bob Mortensen for his dedication in typesetting and his valuable assistance in producing this book. He demonstrated patience, professionalism, and creativity in everything that was produced.

Our deepest appreciation goes to Reeve Love for serving as the editor. She contributed many hours and much love in performing this task.

A warm thank you also goes to Mary Diecker who held together the office in the Third Dimension while the group went on the journey in the Seventh. She also assisted with the cover design and manuscript editing, which helped us to meet our deadlines.

Finally, we wish to thank all thirty-four pioneers who volunteered to make the voyage into the Bermuda Triangle in service to humanity. Without them, this book would not have been possible.

SACRED JOURNEY TO ATLANTIS

TABLE OF CONTENTS

SACRED JOURNEY TO ATLANTIS

PART THREE: THE EXPERIENCE

FOREWORD

THE EXPERIENCE described in this book is a true story. It happened to thirty-four people who are continuing on their paths and, in their own individual ways, working towards the fulfillment of their missions.

We have chosen not to name individuals in order to direct the focus of this story to the power of the whole group experience. However, we want to acknowledge the courage and strength of each one, in a tribute to their abilities to withstand the tests that befall the spiritual warrior on the way to victory. To all of these individuals goes a salute of appreciation, for their hard work, dedication, and commitment to their own healing and transformation in alignment with the greater plan of God.

To the great Beings who supported and guided us on this adventure, and who continue to do so with unceasing love and dedication, we express our boundless gratitude. And to the reader, our sincere desire that this book will inspire you in some way. Should you choose to make this journey back to Atlantis, we hope that the information provided will be of assistance. Our hearts are with you. Bon voyage!

SACRED JOURNEY TO ATLANTIS

A NOTE TO THE READER

THIS BOOK, primarily dictated by the Ascended Masters, is written for the "children of Light" who have come to Earth to fulfill a mission. It contains symbolic messages, the meaning of which will only be revealed to those who meditate on the significance of the words.

The content is like a treasure map. If you, the reader, take it seriously, you could be led to exciting truths and to an understanding of some of the most profound mysteries of the universe. This book is about a journey that has the power to transform life, and it contains a plan for those who wish to venture inward and face the biggest blockage preventing individuals from fulfilling their missions on Earth today—the memory of the destruction of Atlantis. When this memory is confronted, fear is released, causing the soul to move forward with new conviction and dedication to fulfilling its present mission on Earth.

Reading for entertainment is acknowledged as an excellent reason for picking up any book. If that is the motivation for reading this book, however, the reader may be disappointed, for its true power and significance will not be absorbed at that level.

Kuthumi, El Morya, and Delphor, the Ascended Masters who transmitted the messages, have made it clear that to understand the meaning of these messages, one's heart and mind must be disciplined. All the messages are coded, and the decoding is contained within each individual's akashic records. This decoding can be accomplished only by going inward. That means that each message must be studied, meditated upon, and integrated into one's essence. This process takes time, dedication, and a sense of purpose; to commit to the process is a true test of faith. The messages printed on these pages contain the first of several keys that begin to initiate the process.

It has been foretold by prophets and mystics that the lost records of Atlantis would be found at this time in history. It also has been recorded that the mysteries of the ages would be revealed in the Seventh Golden Age. To fulfill these prophecies, a plan was designed by the Ascended Masters.

The plan unfolding on Earth today is so complex that no one person can comprehend it fully. Only the hierarchy of the ascended realms understands the total picture and its intricacies. The overwhelming detail of the multifaceted maneuvers presently being orchestrated is mind-boggling, to say the least. Yet, in spite of its complexity, rest assured that within each soul who has chosen to be a part of this drama is one small piece of the plan. Each piece is equally important and will help complete the puzzle and allow the entire picture to be revealed.

This book holds one piece of that puzzle for those who are destined for membership in the group of 144,000. It contains keys and codes that will assist that group in releasing the fears that are blocking them from remembering the knowledge locked within their akashic records for over 10,000 years. The information transmitted has been lifted from the etheric over Bimini, where the records of Atlantis were sealed when the continent was destroyed. Some of the information provided here actually constitutes the first data that will provide the knowledge needed to control the electron with the power of our minds.

Now is the time for some to *remember* what they already know, and what was taken for granted centuries ago. It is time for some to assume responsibility for unraveling the mysteries of the universe and to implant this knowledge into the structures that support life on Earth.

Knowledge of the mysteries, however, must be earned, says Master Kuthumi, which is why this information is coded. The mysteries contain truths that lead to power. The power cannot be misused again as it once was in Atlantis. The plan decrees that only those souls who have proven worthiness will be granted access to the ancient knowledge or to that level of power again. To prove worthiness, one must discipline the mind and heart and possess a willingness to serve others over self. These are the prerequisites for knowing, and this process takes time. Throughout the learning process, the initiate is watched and guided by the Masters to assure that "right intent" and "right use of will" are present. When all qualifications have been met, transformation occurs.

When individuals are granted an understanding of universal mysteries, they automatically are given greater responsibilities. The assigned roles require the discipline to use the information and power wisely. Consequently, the further one journeys on the path, the narrower the road becomes. The sense of responsibility that one has to self and to others becomes paramount. The more one knows, the more responsibility one is given. The more responsibility one is given, the more service one can provide to others.

The journey we speak of is one of love, Light, mastery, and adventure. It encompasses the Ascended Masters' plan to raise Earth's vibrations through the process of raising our own. The journey is similar to the path the initiates from the mystery schools of Egypt and the elders of Atlantis once practiced, as they brought greater gifts and truths to the world. To embark upon a sacred journey back to Atlantis is to choose to rediscover the secrets to life, abundance, happiness, honesty, and understanding.

SACRED JOURNEY TO ATLANTIS

The journey is guaranteed to be a personal quest, filled with wonder and intrigue. If you are prepared to take this journey and are willing to give the time and to practice the discipline that it will take to walk down this path, this book is for you. It is a manuscript that could change your life.

In reading this book, it is hoped that you will rediscover your connections to the vast, multidimensional levels of consciousness that guide us. We also hope that you will acquire a sharpened perspective as to why our concept of the third dimensional reality must be altered, in order to transcend this plane of consciousness and acquire higher perspectives of what is beyond. More importantly, we hope that you will find answers that will help you unlock your potential, providing you with the direction needed to accomplish your missions.

INTRODUCTION

ATLANTIS IS RISING! That mighty civilization which nurtured some of the greatest minds ever known on Earth is returning, and the effects of its presence will be felt everywhere in the decades to come.

Predictions made in the past stated that by the year 2,000 Atlantis would rise again, like an eagle soaring high in the skies. It would dominate the world for a thousand years, and the effects of its greatness would be experienced everywhere. These predictions were made through eyes trained to see the future. They were made by individuals who experienced glimpses into the Seventh Golden Age, a millennium destined to bring new truths to the world.

The secrets of the Atlantean power are emerging silently today. Full use of the power is destined to be bestowed upon souls who are aligned with Light and love and who understand universal laws. The power, however, will only be given to those who have earned the right to use it. This will assure that the power will not be misused again.

Evidence of the risen Atlantis is everywhere. Many, however, do not recognize the signs even though they are obvious. The signs are:

- ❖ the spiritual awakening encompassing the world;
- ❖ the rapid technological advances being made;
- ❖ the information explosion, doubling knowledge instantly; and

❖ the calmness within the hearts of those who stand silently ready to regain the knowledge needed to control the electron.

The signs that indicate the rising of Atlantis are relatively obvious, but are the signs of the rising Atlantean masters as easy to identify? These souls see through eyes that transcend their physical senses and the illusions around them. They understand their oneness with the unified field of intelligence, and know that in this field of energy, Spirit supports them. Because they know that the physical world has been created through mind energy, and that enlightenment and openmindedness are keys to breaking conceptual constraints set by the world, these masters explore the universe and life from a level of awareness that few on Earth understand today.

Atlantis IS the reincarnated soul who walks silently carrying the knowledge of the highest. Atlantis IS the energy of love, Light, life, and Spirit. It is the mind energy of those who are strong enough to channel only the highest and purest thoughts. Atlantis is alive in those who understand that *thought* is Spirit, and that all form manifests in the physical through the etheric from Spirit.

The Seventh Golden Age will be built through the minds and hearts of those who walk united with Spirit. They are the souls who have forsaken ego and replaced it with the will of God. They are the souls who are programmed with the desire to fulfill their missions of bringing everlasting peace and harmony to Earth. They are the peacemakers who live to assist in ushering forth the Age of Aquarius.

The time is at hand for the Atlantean spirit to rise and again meet the challenge of becoming victorious in the quest to:

Become one with God.

As Master Kuthumi has stated:

> *This requires balancing the male and female ener-
> gies within, and controlling those energies through
> a focused approach of uniting the heart, mind, and
> will. Oneness requires that ego be displaced for the
> will of God. Oneness with the God Force enables all
> to perform miracles, which has been humanity's
> birthright from the beginning. In short, oneness
> must be remembered, to enable us to "BE" what we
> already are.*

This challenge to achieve oneness will be the standard
for the millennium. This standard was momentarily forgotten after the cataclysmic events surrounding the fall
of Atlantis tore humanity from its connection to the Divine.

The spirit of Atlantis has not risen before because the
vibrations on Earth were not conducive, until now, to
support the return of the Atlantean souls, programmed to
rebuild the glory of that earlier time. Even today, worldwide conditions hardly match the accomplishments
remembered in the mind's eye of the Atlantean master.
It will be that memory, however, that will guide these
individuals to create greatness once again.

Now, with the dawning of the Age of Aquarius, our
wait to reclaim our understanding of this ancient knowledge is coming to an end. The Age of Pisces opened the
heart centers of all who grew weary of the pain and suffering that period brought. The new millennium stands
waiting to reveal its secrets of mastery and love. Those
destined to lead and teach the masses are the souls who
have returned to Earth by choice, to usher in a new wave
of consciousness that will truly create Heaven on Earth.

Those who will reclaim the power of the fifth dimensional human are those who walk the Earth today unre-
stricted by old paradigms of limitation. Surfacing from

their souls is a remembrance of life in a different form. They are remembering creation, not limitation. They remember life, not death. They are ridding their cellular, genetic, and akashic record memory banks of all negativity, allowing truths encoded within the frequencies of Light and sound to break through.

In the next two decades much on Earth will crumble and will have to be reborn. In the rebirth process, old systems that have failed will not be restored. In their place will come developments based upon higher frequencies and upon the Atlantean codes. When the time is right, the masters who have been carefully prepared through many lifetimes will assume the responsibility of rebuilding.

All Atlantean souls intuitively know that they must earn the right to reclaim the knowledge they once possessed in that former civilization. To achieve this right involves a quest to synchronize the mind, heart, and will. There is no other way, say Kuthumi and El Morya, for masters must prove their worthiness. To regain this level of knowledge, each must be tested. Should the power be misused again, the road to destruction would close the evolutionary doors on Earth for another 26,000 years.

The vision for Earth is an event unprecedented in the heavens. We are embarking on a journey into the Seventh Golden Age which no other prerecorded age can rival. If we believe that the accomplishments of Egypt or Greece were phenomenal, we must now stand watch to witness even greater events yet to come. This new era will lead the inhabitants of the world to a threshold of greatness, attained only through a universal understanding of the oneness of All.

To understand oneness, one first must think of the universe as everlasting, having no beginning or end. When we shift our own internal paradigms to look at the world and the universe from this unified approach, we begin to see ourselves as an integral part of this perfection. As such, we are one with this intelligence and energy field. Only our egos keep us separated from experiencing this. Separation sets limitations, and in these limitations we experience that all is not perfect, whole, and in harmony.

The spirit of Atlantis remembers that oneness is the key to creation. The Atlantean souls know that the paths to higher creation and to the Seventh Golden Age require all to become enlightened beings. Once realized, limitations dissolve, and creation becomes limitless.

When an individual is one with the unified energy field, and learns to reject limitation, then that individual begins to move into the new frontier of the mind. This book is designed to take you on a journey into the mind. It contains messages that require decoding, through meditation and contemplation. If one wishes to learn the mysteries within the messages, one must apply discipline and effort, and access inner spaces to retrieve understanding.

Right use of will is the key to mastery. Therefore, the information retrieved by disciplining oneself and committing to this process is of little value to the soul who wishes only to gratify ego. Atlantean masters understand how futile the process is if will is not aligned with the Higher Self. Spirit guides all souls who walk into the millennium, and it is through Spirit that peace, harmony, and abundance will be restored to the beloved Terra.

The information within these messages resonates with frequencies, says Kuthumi. All is vibration. The vibratory frequencies that reach one individual will not be the same for another. The messages are magical, for they bring forth perfect understanding for each who studies them. Studying this book is truly an exercise in journeying into the Fifth Dimension, for the mind is destined to expand from this process.

SACRED JOURNEY TO ATLANTIS

Until one is committed, there is hesitancy, the chance to draw back, always ineffectiveness, concerning all acts of initiative (and creation).

There is one elementary truth, the ignorance of which kills countless ideas & splendid plans: that the moment one definitely commits oneself, then providence moves too. All sorts of things occur to help one that would never otherwise have occurred.

A whole stream of events issues from the decision, raising in one's favor all manner of unforeseen incidents & meetings & material assistance which no person could have dreamed would have come his way.

Whatever you can do or dream you can, begin it.

Boldness has genius, power & magic in it.

Begin it now.

Goethe

CHAPTER I:
THE SEED IS PLANTED

A **SPIRITUAL** awakening is occurring on Earth that was predicted thousands of years ago. Individuals everywhere are being touched by higher energies channeled to Earth at this time to assist in a rebirthing process. This awakening provides each person opportunities to choose the most appropriate path and to live a life of higher truths, values, and integrity.

The awakening affects individuals in different ways. Some choose to "clean up their acts" by letting go of situations that have caused them pain. Some rediscover God and experience the sense of love that this rediscovery brings. Others direct their energies in service to the world, such as helping humanity or cleansing the Earth, which needs so much attention. Still others travel to sacred power spots around the globe, channelling higher vibrations into the very essence of the Earth's core and experiencing transformation in the process.

The uniqueness of each path is programmed by the Higher Self. What is "right" for one is not necessarily right for another. Each path is different, yet all lead to the same goal—enlightenment.

Enlightenment implies understanding. As used in this text, enlightenment represents an illumined state of mind achieved through mastery and through initiations which challenge individuals to seek higher truths, values, and consciousness. The achievement of enlightenment usually takes years and requires discipline and dedication.

A seeker of illumination is often called a student, disciple, or initiate, and eventually is guided by great Beings of Light who are called Ascended Masters. These Masters are our elder sisters and brothers who have walked before us and who light the way for those in embodiment on the Earth plane. Some of the great Masters commonly known to all are Jesus, the Buddha, Zoroaster, Mother Mary, Krishna, and Quan Yin. These are but a few who guide us now, for there are many. In reality, there are countless numbers who assist us on our journey to know God.

The goal of enlightenment is for individuals to become Masters in physical form. Few have accomplished this in the past because of the dedication, purity, and commitment that it takes to do so. Yet, just as those in the ascended realms have managed to accomplish this feat by mastering the Earth's curriculum of love, Light, and an understanding of universal laws, so shall we in time. Only through mastery shall each of us walk in the footsteps of those who have gone before.

Enlightenment prepares us for entry into a world and kingdom foreign to Earth's existence. This new world is in the Fifth Dimension and higher. It is a world of thought manifestation and one which knows no boundaries such as we experience here on Earth. Understanding the laws that govern this higher state of existence requires a higher consciousness and an understanding of a language that is transmitted primarily through analogies and symbolism. To excel in learning this new curriculum requires one to transcend the understanding of the physical, three-dimensional world in which we live. It demands that one accept a viewpoint of existence from a totally different perspective—a viewpoint which is often one hundred and eighty degrees at variance from the one which we have accepted as truth.

Since Earth is a physical, dense world, everything here is experienced through the five senses. Thus, we witness life from the perspective that everything is either a solid, liquid, or gas. In higher dimensions, energy vibrates at a higher frequency, closer to the speed of light. There, the *etheric* governs existence. The rules and procedures are very different, making it difficult to understand except through the use of symbols and analogies. To describe it would be like seeing a color never seen on Earth before and trying to explain that color to a friend. Or, to use a more common example, it would be like trying to describe a color to someone without eyesight.

It is through the higher dimensions and an understanding of them, however, that humans will find freedom from limitation. Understanding the curricula of higher dimensions will free us from the pain and suffering which have kept us in bondage for so long. It is through this portal of time/space that many on Earth are preparing to become Masters, transcending the limitations that hold us to the past and prevent us from seeing the future.

The journey to mastery begins from within. It is a spiritual journey on a path that gets narrower and narrower. When one decides to undertake the journey, he or she automatically agrees to be a participant in a program designed to strengthen the soul.

Mastery *is* the path to enlightenment. It is the decision to leave worldly possessions in the Third Dimension behind in search of the gifts of the higher dimensions of love and Light. Mastery is the approach one takes to find the power from within, which ends the search for the power from around. It represents the culmination of the journey that leads to peace of mind, harmony, abundance, and love.

The journey to higher consciousness lies within each of us. It is a journey that usually takes years to achieve, yet can be attained by any soul who wishes to undertake the experience. The journey can be painless, although it is sometimes through experiencing pain that growth occurs. The journey is free, although it is through

4

giving (as the initiate learns) that the real benefits and rewards are received—tenfold and more. The journey is priceless, which no one who has undergone the experience will deny.

The journey on which the Ascended Masters guide individuals is one which involves: diversity, yet oneness; separateness, then unity with the Higher Self; testing, but with strict integrity; unconditional love, compassion, and forgiveness; patience and acceptance; freedom, yet discipline; and commitment. If one is ready to acquire these characteristics and learn what they mean in the higher realms, then one is ready to walk the path of the spiritual warrior and begin the journey to enlightenment.

The story recorded in this book describes only part of a journey that each individual who travelled to Bimini has taken in this lifetime. The events detailed here tell of one challenge posed to each person. The events also represent the culmination of several tests of initiation that have been experienced thus far by each.

The decision to go on the trip was a personal one for each in attendance. The learning experienced was also individualized. The Ascended Masters never told us what we should or should not do—that is not their style, nor is it their role. In fact, to do so would be contrary to their essence. They made suggestions and guided us—that is all. We were always free to choose whatever direction we wished to take.

The suggestion to make the "Sacred Journey to Atlantis" was actually made nearly a full year prior to the trip, *although at that time no one suspected that the foundation was being laid for the trip to Bimini.* The seed was planted in a message received by Norma Milanovich from Master Kuthumi, requesting that she and her husband, Rudy, consider taking a trip to England and Egypt. Neither of them had ever considered travelling to sacred sites or power points. During the previous years they had met individuals who had done so and were always interested in hearing about the experiences, but had not considered this a part of their own lifestyle.

Messages began to be transmitted telepathically to Norma during the winter of 1990 suggesting that they might wish to consider taking a trip to England and Egypt. While this seemed appealing, it also seemed impractical, for they did not have the money for such a trip. Also, they were concerned about the time it would take. With both of them working, it seemed inconvenient to take two weeks for a trip that did not fulfill either a business purpose or the desire to visit family members.

For three months these thoughts persisted. Finally, on March 18th, Norma sat at the computer and asked Kuthumi for clarification as to why this trip was even being suggested. Over a period of months she received several transmissions which clarified the purpose and agenda.

It quickly became clear that there was a much higher purpose for this trip and that it had to do with accessing power points on Earth. As usual, Kuthumi's responses were both humbling and intriguing. The very essence of the messages changed their initial attitudes about going.

Entire sections from each of the messages are reprinted below. At first glance, it may appear that these messages are not directly related to this book, which is a summary of the trip to Bimini. Studying them, however, reveals other information, of great importance, within the words. While the messages were specific to two individuals, they also contain important general information for anyone wishing to travel to sacred places. For example, they reveal the nature of the exchange of energies that takes place within individuals when they access sacred spots. In other cases, instructions are given that detail procedures to follow when entering certain vortexes or temples. Also, the benefits that humanity receives when one enters these power areas are revealed; thus, the rationale for completing such journeys is outlined.

SACRED JOURNEY TO ATLANTIS

As an individual contemplates a trip to a sacred energy vortex, he or she must know that there is always a higher purpose for going there. That higher purpose encompasses destiny, mission, attainment of higher truths, and/or spiritual growth. Often these reasons are not understood or even acknowledged as the reasons for making such a trip. We might believe that we are planning a three-week vacation to sightsee in the Andes of Peru, when, in reality, the Higher Self is guiding us there for a much higher purpose, incomprehensible to the rational mind.

We hope that the information contained in the following messages on England, Egypt, and Greece, which actually set the stage for the journey to Bimini, will provide the foundation for understanding the messages and information presented later in this book. It is a fascinating process to witness how perfectly orchestrated everything really is. Hindsight gives one the power to see the connections that were being made; and, in retrospect, it is clear that these initial messages were setting the stage and providing the training program for the journey yet to come—Bimini!

March 18, 1990

KUTHUMI, I SURROUND MYSELF WITH LOVE AND LIGHT AND REQUEST A TRANSMISSION FROM YOU THIS MORNING. PLEASE GIVE RUDY AND ME CLARIFICATION REGARDING THE TRIP TO ENGLAND AND EGYPT. ALSO, PLEASE PROVIDE A TENTATIVE AGENDA AND THE AMOUNT OF TIME YOU SUGGEST WE STAY IN EACH OF THE COUNTRIES.

Good morning, Bright Star.

We send you greetings from the realms of the Highest, and welcome you back to the fold. It has been some time since we have completed a communication of this nature, and we thank you for providing us the opportunity again to make the connection. Again it is I, Kuthumi, your Father and Guide for your journey on the Earth plane in this moment of time.

The journey to England and Egypt is significant for your path and Rudy's. It is important because of the tremendous currents of energy being stirred up in those areas of the world. You and Rudy have chosen the path of the spiritual warrior in this lifetime; and it is because you have done so that you are destined to "trouble" many of the cries that are beginning to surge over the beloved Terra.

The journey to England and the Nile is designed specifically for that reason. By appearing in selected energy vortexes, you will channel a higher vibrational current into the sacred areas which will help activate the mysteries destined to be revealed. Also, your presence will allow you access to etheric records that have lain dormant for eons of time. By giving to the Earth and the plan, you will be receivers. In receiving, you will be wiser. By obtaining wisdom, you will see the glory and magnificence of the God Force.

Take the journey with your heart center and third eye in constant equilibrium. Go with the Spirit of God, and allow Spirit to guide your many steps. Do not take an agenda. Instead, allow things to fall into place the way the moment moves you.

In both places proceed with ease and enjoyment. If you feel a yearning or pulling of your Spirit at any given moment, allow that moment to guide you. We tell you that this will provide more knowledge and wisdom than any plan you could develop.

While in England, drive to the southern coast and stay one evening on the shore that connects that country to the mainland of Europe. [Rudy and Norma interpreted this site to be Dover, which was confirmed in the second message.] *Bring the energy of Stonehenge and Glastonbury with you to this location. Therefore, I suggest that you take this journey last. Meditate in all areas you visit, especially on the hillside of Glastonbury. Walk the paths of the Druids and access their codes on the etheric. Command that the highest memories come forth from these moments and relive that which you created so many centuries ago in your Earth time.*

Remember the Thames. Remember the Thames. The rivers of England that comprise its banner are significant for the memory of St. George. Take the memory and move its significance to Glastonbury, allowing at all times the two to become one in this moment of time. Should you be successful in doing this, the future will be yours. I say no more.

When you journey down the Nile, take the moment of truth that each of you experienced as Initiates of Isis, and command that it return with your presence. Access the tombs and energy spots that are still sacred today. As you move through them, open your third eye chakra to obtain the wisdom that is waiting to be unleashed. When passing through those spots to other points on your journey, close your inner doors to retain the sacred information in an urn within your solar plexus area. Capture its essence as you would the most precious perfumes and oils. Then allow the aroma to stay for a brief moment before depositing it within the solar plexus area, where, following this experience, it will be positioned for immediate use in years to come.

SACRED JOURNEY TO ATLANTIS

The main focal points of your visit to Egypt shall be, and forever will be, the Great Pyramid of Giza and the Temple of Isis. They will initiate and culminate the journey on the etheric, for they represent the total combining of male and female electromagnetic energy forces in operation on the Earth today. While the structures are still activated, they can no longer perform the duties of the Command, because of the distortions and misrepresentations that have manifested in these areas throughout the ages. Therefore, journey there with shields up, and allow only the purest of energies to siphon through your gauze.

We shall provide more information on the details in the days to come. For today, this introduction seems to suffice. Study it well before you fly to your destiny.

You asked about the length of time. It is written that you will stay for seven days in England and nine in Egypt. There is significance to these numbers and for the world. Heed them carefully and enjoy, my Beloved Daughter and Son of the Command.

I AM Kuthumi. Adonai.

What can one say upon receiving a message such as this? Naturally, the message changed Norma's and Rudy's attitudes about going. It sounded fascinating, although they hardly understood a word that had been transmitted. What did Kuthumi mean when he said that "It is written that you will stay for seven days in England and nine in Egypt?" Did that preclude free choice and imply destiny? In the Far East the Masters refer to these turning points in life as dharma. Were Norma and Rudy about to embark on a major turning point in their lives? And, if so, did that mean that journeying to special power vortexes on Earth had the power to alter anyone's life, moving people closer to their missions and destiny? The entire premise of this book implies just that.

Shortly after providing this message, in another transmission, Kuthumi stated the following:

In April of this year, an etheric door is opening over the Nile. In this opening all the lost records of Egypt and the ancient scriptures for that civilization are being activated. It is likened to a library vault that has been closed for centuries, and the doors to this great chamber are once again being unlocked.

To travel there while this portal of time/space is open will allow you to be programmed with the information you will need to fulfill your mission on Earth. It will provide you with the information, keys, and codes necessary to understand Egypt's connection to the Templar.[1] The etheric doorway will only be opened for six months. We are guiding several Starseeds there to celebrate the opening of the portal, and we request that you journey there to seal this gateway.

For several weeks Norma and Rudy studied the messages, asking friends for input. Three other individuals stated that they felt compelled to join them in Egypt, which they did. Six months later, the same three persons were also among the thirty-four who journeyed to Bimini. Thus, five of the thirty-four shared this journey by experiencing the energies of both Egypt and Bimini. Rudy and Norma initiated the process in England and Greece.

In June, several weeks after the messages had been received, it appeared to be time to obtain more information regarding this trip. The energies were in motion to go, individuals were committed, and plans were being formed. England appeared to be the first stop, which was where Rudy and Norma would start the journey. The five would meet in Cairo on a designated date. Norma returned to the computer to ask Kuthumi for additional input. The message zeroed in on the first part of the trip—England.

June 2, 1990

KUTHUMI, I REQUEST TO BE ALLOWED TO RE-ESTABLISH A CONNECTION TO YOUR FREQUENCY AND RECEIVE ANOTHER TRANSMISSION. IN LIGHT AND LOVE I ASK THAT YOU SEND ME FURTHER INFORMATION REGARDING OUR TRIP TO ENGLAND.

Greetings, Oh Daughter of the Command.

It is I, Kuthumi, coming to your side this evening to honor your request. I am pleased to provide you with more detailed information regarding your journey to Great Britain.

The journey must come in two parts. The first part must include the direction toward the west, where you will re-discover the energy of the Command as it was initiated over two thousand years ago. There you will experience the energy of the Grail and the tribute to the Most Radiant One.

We recommend you avail yourselves of each location that directs you to the remembrances of the Holy Grail and Arthurian legend. This is of prime importance on this trip, for it is in these vortexes of the Divine that you will discover the necessary steps that link your beingness with the design of the Templar.

The second part of the journey must conclude in Dover. There you will receive a shot in the arm, so to speak, as you participate in the etheric victory of the courageous ones, who initiated that point into action nearly fifty years ago. The current of energy there has been reactivated in recent months. The etheric is now ready to project patriotism, honor, courage, and dedication into your akashic records. You both will experience a programming on the etheric that you will not forget. This journey will contain the boost of perseverance you both have been waiting to receive.

On your way it would prove wise and worthy to stop in Canterbury, for there is much wisdom that can be assimilated from that stop, as well. The majic [sic] of this location is still alive. Perhaps you might even experience the delight of your lives in this location. That remains for you to determine and create if you recognize the opportunities and occurrences once you have arrived.

The knowledge of Stonehenge must be restored to the world. It must be taken seriously; therefore, your time in this location must consist of a minimum of thirty minutes. This time will allow the Masters to work within your shields to program you with the codes[2] necessary for connecting the Templar with the heavens.[3] The star systems that made that monument the glorious achievement it is are still alive in the heavens. Recapture that knowledge and move only clockwise around its structure as you approach. This will allow the perfect alignment of energy currents to connect to the neuron structures within your etheric bodies. In this motion of energy you will not upset your DNA and RNA flow of electrons. Following these procedures will only enhance the strength of the currents.[4]

We cannot stress these directions enough. It is also imperative that you journey to Stonehenge first. This will prepare you for the rest of the journey, as it will establish *the motion for your programming that will continue for the entire trip.*

The Thames is important, for it connects the past to the present. It represents the journey of the soul in its Light Body as it moves from the source to the Creator of the All. The water will give you strength, right from the beginning. Wash your hands in its liquid, should you get the opportunity. The renewal will bring you truth and fresh commitment to England and all that she has stood for from the beginning of time.

Glastonbury will be the highlight for the renewal of the vows to the Command. It will bring life to the blood that is in your veins and will announce to the world that the beginning and the end are all in this moment of time. Access the many points that renew the legends of Arthur and Merlin. Take advantage of the hillsides that you once meditated upon, so many centuries ago. Believe in your hearts that this moment is the truth, and all truths shall be revealed to you.

This concludes the agenda for the journey soon to commence.

We stress again that this journey is one of utmost importance for the future of planet Earth. It takes the plan from the etheric to the physical dimensions of time/space. We will walk beside you every step of the way.

Listen to your inner commands, Dearhearts, and move with the Divine. The path is glorious and straight once you complete this challenge and adventure in August and September of your Earth year.

I remain your Father and Guide. I AM Kuthumi. Adonai.

With the second message, everything became even more suspenseful. Both messages were filled with mystery and intrigue. It was clear that Kuthumi was a master of psychology as he wove the symbolism, keys, and codes within the lines that provided direction for the trip.

To interpret the full significance of each message, Norma would have had to ask Kuthumi hundreds of questions, which she knew she did not have time to do. Also, knowing Kuthumi's writing style, and the fact that his title is World Teacher, made her aware that to undertake such a process would be fruitless. While he undoubtedly would answer each question with great fluency and eloquence, each new answer also would be presented in such a way that she and Rudy would have to figure out the meaning on their own. Kuthumi has not earned the title of World Teacher without good reason.

It is Kuthumi's job to empower individuals on Earth and to assist them to become Masters. All good teachers understand the importance of not giving away answers too easily to students. Making the students use their own minds and exercise intuition is the process that all excellent teachers use when empowering others. Kuthumi is an excellent teacher.

Therefore, Norma and Rudy were placed in the position of two people with a treasure map, trying to discover the clues that would lead them to the treasure. When enough time had elapsed and they had exhausted their own interpretations of what Kuthumi had meant in the message on England, Norma returned to the computer and requested information regarding another segment of the trip, Egypt.

July 1, 1990

KUTHUMI, I WELCOME YOUR TRANSMISSION THIS EVENING. PLEASE COME THROUGH AND PROVIDE

SACRED JOURNEY TO ATLANTIS

ME WITH ADDITIONAL INFORMATION ON THE
JOURNEY TO EGYPT.

Good evening, Oh Daughter of Light.

*I thank you for honoring my request, and I will indeed
take this opportunity to provide you and yours with
additional information on your upcoming journey to
Egypt.*

*The journey will be one of much excitement and dread.
The excitement will come from your reliving the past and
remembering the events you once created. The dread will
come from the heat, so we request you surround yourself
with much blue. If you do, you will not notice the intensity as much as you believe you will now. Trust me, as
I speak truth.*

*The journey from Aswan will include reliving the past
and creating the future all in one moment of time. It will
culminate with a tour of the Temples of Luxor and Karnak,
and will provide details you will need when you return.
Take the information given in these areas seriously, for
there is a coding there to understand that awaits your
interpretation of the symbolism.*

*In these areas, please note the colors used inside the
temples and tombs. Know that these were powerful
vortexes in their day, and that they symbolized entry to
other dimensions of time/space. These magical works
were designed by the gods to be placed where all knowledge was restored and provided for eternity. In this civilization there were many truths that cannot be denied,
even today.*

*The symbolism you will experience will be of a different
kind when you arrive in these locations. The symbols will*

contain a special vibration that is such that, if you medi-
tate on them, your inner consciousness will move doors
that block your present-day consciousness from retrieving
them. The symbols there will reunite the Spirit of your
Higher Selves with the physical world in which you live.
They will decode the meaning of life and will provide the
direction you need to accomplish the building of the
Templar.

This is truth also.

Take this part of the journey more seriously than any
other part of the tour. Know that you will have been
prepared in the Temple of Isis and that the molecular
structure that contains your genetic memory will have
been redesigned. Know that all the information acquired
after visiting the Temple of Isis will be that which is
necessary to fulfill your missions in this lifetime. You
will understand once you are there. You will also know
the meaning of life, as it will be fulfilled within the days
to follow.

The journey into the Great Pyramid of Giza will cul-
minate the journey. It is fitting that you and the
others should make your final ascensions toward
your mission in this part of the world and in the vortex
that created the Master on Earth.[5] Know that it is still
active, but not to the degree that it was many centuries
ago. This is not of consequence, for the energies from
within will reactivate the souls. Take the respect that you
once knew in that former lifetime to these points. Remem-
ber the calling and the programming from the God
Force that describes your obligation to the people
of Earth. Know that the plan is being fulfilled and
that you and the others are once again journeying to
the highest point of consciousness that the world can
offer.

In this journey allow yourselves the opportunity to understand how the people of Egypt live today, and thank them for their simple ways. Know that they are truly the keepers of this energy, and that it is their dedication that has made all this possible for you and the others to go there. Know that they will remember when they see you. There is much to say about this, but at a later time.

I say no more on this matter for now. I only wish to allow you the time to contemplate these words.

Thank you again, my colleague of the Command, for honoring my request. I retire now and send you the love and admiration of the entire Galactic Fleet.

Adonai.

Approximately two weeks later another transmission was received giving further clarification on the upcoming trip.

July 13, 1990

KUTHUMI, I SURROUND MYSELF WITH LIGHT AND LOVE AND REQUEST THAT YOU SEND THROUGH ANOTHER TRANSMISSION ON OUR TRIP TO ENGLAND, GREECE, AND EGYPT.

Dearest Daughter in the Light. I, Kuthumi, am transmitting this message this evening in the midst of the washing away of negativity.[6] It is significant that this ocean of cleansing is upon you, for this marks a day in the heavens where you and many others will soon experience a great decrease in the annoyances that have plagued you for the past several months. This is said to inform you that you are now cloaked with a protective shield not

18

experienced before. This protection will assure safe passage through the next decade.

This shield is extended to all who are awakened as of this date. It is extended to each soul who seeks the Light in the name of the Most Radiant One. It is the honor and the badge of the Command, and you will soon discover that the protection is real and that it will promote many good tidings of great joy for the children of Light.

This protection could not be bestowed upon the souls until the Earth's vibrational frequency had registered a certain mark in the heavens. As of this date, that mark has been reached, through the constant dedication of the children of the Command. You have wandered for many long fortnights and yearned for peace. We announce to you that it will now come in the increments that you have so desired.

This shift of energy levels and protection must be explained, for it relates to the upcoming journey of the group. This frequency and shield will prepare all of the children to be better receivers of information and messages when they tour the temples and tombs of the great ones. The rebirth of the New Age has truly begun as of this evening in time, and in this remembering the sapphire stones of the hierarchy have been positioned in the etheric body structures of the Light bodies. Take this information to your hearts, Oh Children of the Nile. Know that this moment is indeed rare and one which will surpass everything that has preceded it. Walk with liberty and with grace, just as you once did as you danced on the shores of the water and body that gave the world life.

The connection to the present and past in this moment of time will be your experience in Greece. It will assume the

19

midpoint of the journey[7] for you to understand the connection of the present moment of power to the ancient ones of the great worlds. The Oracle of Delphi will give you wisdom beyond compare, for the energy vortex of Apollo awaits to be reawakened to the soul who will be able to channel this energy once again. The tripod that existed within this delta is one which is still active in the etheric. It has not connected to a voice that has brought through the ancient ones since before the coming of the great Master, Jesus. The drought has been effective. Now we await to hear the cries of the Highest as they provide you the opportunity to bring through messages from the Grecian triumph as well as the Egyptian one.

The connection between these great civilizations is not as clear in your written documents as it is in the master plan for the universe. These two great worlds took the best of both worlds and melted them into the directions of the seen and unseen. For the Earth's progression, it is necessary to understand both directions and the gifts that they bring.

In Greece, the ancient ones used power from the Fifth Dimension to manifest physical worlds as you know them to be. In Egypt, the great ones took the powers of the Fifth Dimension and higher and mastered the connection to the hidden worlds and the link to the Higher Selves. In your world and the New Golden Age approaching, it is the duty of the star children to walk the paths of both worlds, and to link the Higher Selves with the physical world through the hidden dimensions of the soul and inner worlds. Know this to be true.

Your journey to Greece will awaken manifestation powers you have longed to understand. It will also provide you the opportunity to speak to Apollo, should you choose to *take advantage of this opportunity while in Delphi. Take this message seriously, and follow the commands with great dignity and duty.*

Approach the point of power, where the Oracle of Delphi was the voice of the ancient ones, with much respect. Call upon the voice of the Sirens and hear the calling of Apollo. Beckon the great one to come with softness and surrender to that point of power. Allow the energy of the Grecian Oracle to sit beside you in a meditative state. Request that the code for the future be brought to your consciousness.

If you should do this, the code shall be delivered. If you should do this, know that you automatically assume the responsibility to be a messenger for Apollo. Do not take this assignment lightly, Dearest Commander. Few have been asked to be the voice of Greece and the gifts that it brought to the world. There are many hidden secrets from this etheric world, just as there are many in Egypt. Know that the voice of the great ones will guide you on your path, and do not fear.

By the time you travel to Egypt, the energies of the planet will have been raised to a level not ever seen before. Only this condition will allow for the greater communications [described earlier] to flow. This was not possible before this time, for the frequencies of the children of Light were not strong enough to receive the higher voice of God. All is quickly changing within the next forty-five days. Learn of the benefits in the days and months to come. There are many gifts for you as you continue to bring these words through for others. We hope that you will soon see the benefits, and will move to dedicate more of your time to bring through these messages for the world.

21

*Good night, Commander, in the name of the Radiant One.
I say good health also, for it is coming to you soon.*

It is I, Kuthumi, bidding you a pleasant evening. Adonai.

The messages served to increase the anxiety and anticipation of the group. The suspense kept building, creating additional concerns. One evening, a group member called to say that she had heard that it was dangerous to meditate in the King's Chamber overnight, something that the group had contemplated doing. Not knowing how to respond to this, or if it was even true, they decided to contact Kuthumi for some guidance on this matter.

The answer was a surprise, as so many of Kuthumi's responses are. Here is what he said:

July 29, 1990

KUTHUMI, PLEASE SURROUND ME WITH LOVE AND LIGHT AND SEND THROUGH ANOTHER TRANSMISSION. ONE OF THE GROUP MEMBERS HAS STATED THAT SHE HEARD IT CAN BE DANGEROUS TO MEDITATE IN THE KING'S CHAMBER. IS THIS SO?

Greetings, Oh Daughter of Light.

I am here with you this evening to answer your important question. I will begin with a parable that may sound familiar on another level of reality.

In a land far away, there once lived an old man who took great pride in using his mental energies to manifest anything his heart desired. He focused on his desires for the day, and with great dedication moved the forces of nature to provide whatever gave him comfort and glory. He used this power to secure that which only benefitted himself, and cared little for the masses.

In the course of his days he became very lonely, for his friends became tired of his selfishness. They gave him little comfort because he took many problems and concerns of his greed to them. They also felt little sympathy for his dilemma. In short, he did not receive, for he did not give.

When it came time for him to die he passed on to other dimensions of reality. He looked back on his lifetime and wondered what he would have done differently if he had not been given the power. In his final analysis he decided that what he should have done was to use the power for others and not for himself. If he had done that, all would have been returned to him in manyfold returns, but he did not understand that in the flesh.

Although he understood this lesson on the akashic record level, he knew that it would take many lifetimes to understand the full intent of its meaning and rewards. Therefore, he decided to take the journey in the next lifetime in Egypt, which would give him the opportunity to learn.

In his next embodiment as a fair woman, his soul visited the Great Pyramid to allow the power to unfold again. To her amazement, she found that the power did not unfold at the level her soul remembered. She experienced a struggle from within and discovered a blockage to that which she wished to reclaim as her heritage.

When she entered the King's Chamber, she was brought back into such loneliness and despair that she could not recover from the experience. She found that her memory of the former lifetime was so strong that it allowed all the memories to surface to be experienced again. This is the secret of the King's Chamber. Entering this area provides a powerful moment, but especially for those who come prepared.

If you enter this area surrounded with negative thoughts from the past, the magnitude of the energy is bound to fulfill all the experiences tenfold. This can cause problems that are difficult to recover from. The chamber contains one of the most powerful vortexes of energy available to humans on Earth.

If one knows this and is awakened, one is certain to know how to protect oneself. If you go thinking of futuristic thoughts and focusing on God and enlightenment, that will certainly be yours. The experience then will accelerate your path. If the thoughts within your own hidden chambers are reliving former, unpleasant dreams, then these will consume you.

Your protection is the Light. It is as simple as that. You need not fear anything. Know only that what you focus your thoughts on is what you will manifest intently and quickly.

Experience the entire trip from Aswan to the Pyramid as though you were reliving the most delightful time of your lives. Remember the ancient mysteries and truths. Recall the peace and glory that was once yours. Hear the inner voices of wisdom that guide and salute your return. Then, enter the King's Chamber with the full presence of your Higher Selves and request that the transformation occur to your Higher Selves and mission. This will be our promise and delight.

Thank you for allowing me this opportunity to explain this to you. Go in peace, Dear One.

I AM Kuthumi. Adonai.

Shortly after receiving this message, the world situation escalated and we appeared to be on the brink of war in the Middle East. While that war did not actually begin until nearly six months later, the thought of going into Egypt during the intensification of the conflict presented Rudy, Norma, and the other three with many challenges and tests of faith. Suddenly, their earlier fascination with the journey had taken on another significance.

Friends who knew nothing of the messages were urging them not to go. Some were suggesting that they wait and play it safe—postpone the trip until all conditions settled down. They were scheduled to leave near the end of August and the conflict was intensifying daily. They asked for guidance in one, final message, and Kuthumi sent the following words through, just prior to their leaving.

August 23, 1990

KUTHUMI, I SURROUND MYSELF WITH LOVE AND LIGHT AND REQUEST THAT YOU SEND ME ANOTHER TRANSMISSION REGARDING OUR TRIP TO GREECE AND EGYPT.

Dearest Daughter in the Light of Our Most Radiant One.

I, Kuthumi, come through this frequency to provide you with assurances and love that no harm will come to you on your journey for the Command. It has been requested of you to take this journey at this time for the purpose of providing the beloved Terra with great wisdom and Light. In your travels you will notice that your courage and dedication to the Command will not, in any way, deceive you. The journey will be one of peace, happiness, and harmony during a time of strife, anger, and trickery. Yours will be the path of the Divine walked among those who travel paths of deception. Both you and Rudy have tremendous courage and are admired for your strength and commitment. You have completed similar journeys in different lifetimes. It is at this time that you draw strength from the remembrances of those former, courageous days.

Take the itinerary that was provided to you with you on the journey. Note the suggestions we made and make the best use of your time in the relaxing and meditative states. This will maximize the opportunity for enlightenment and joy.

We stand watch and protect you both. We also wash the path in front of you wherever you travel. Know that truth will set you free. The world needs the courage of the Commanders. The world must be set free by the star children who know no fear. This is a true test of courage and a measure of mastery over fear.

You both have found that your powers of manifestation are increasing. In this knowingness you understand that the laws we have taught are indeed true. Stay in your centeredness at all times and open your minds and hearts to many.

Many lives will be touched by the energies of your Higher Selves. Know this and take the journey seriously as you walk the path of your former days in Egypt. See the Light all around, and consciously place the Light within the temples and sacred places everywhere you go.

The trek in Egypt will not be that which you visualize. You will understand more than you consciously realize at this moment. Hear and read the signs of the times around and learn to register the impressions within your subconscious. If you should do this, you will have mastered the path of Sananda, who walked that valley so many years before. He understood the terror and the anguish of the people of Earth. He knew that only truth sets you free.

You also must live your truths and know that the world awaits the Commanders who master truth to walk the shores of the Nile once again.

Carry the banner of the Command with you wherever you go. Understand that the vision of the Highest is what will guide you through all of your coming days.

When I said in the earlier months of your year that after June your life would not be the same, did you ever expect to see such unforeseen circumstances? Consider this to be not a test of vibrational love, but instead a test of commitment to the Command. Know that your courage will gain high honors on the path and the world will gain much in frequency for your dedication and efforts.

Each soul is measured by the contributions it makes. Each soul contains immense power and love, and has the capabilities of ruling the world. All know that their destinies are to serve, but few understand that they have the opportunity to be selected.

Walk the journey with confidence and Light. We will guide each step until you discover the truths and realize that you never needed us to guide you in the first place. The divinity within all of you is intense and beautiful. The Light from within is truly the source of power for the world. If all understood this the way you are beginning to, there would be no war or hardship on your beautiful planet.

Go in peace and share the bread of life. I now close this communication, but look forward to meeting you on the etheric in the Temple of Love this evening.

SACRED JOURNEY TO ATLANTIS

Adonai, my children and Commanders. I AM your dedicated Father and Teacher for the next several weeks. We shall relive many happy moments together. Adonai.

Kuthumi's words were comforting and encouraging, but anxiety levels were still a little elevated. This journey was a true test of courage and commitment. The five friends met the night before Rudy and Norma left for England to discuss last minute details. Interestingly enough, when the world situation was discussed all five admitted that they were experiencing an inner sense of calmness they had not understood before. That was significant for them all, and made the trip easier.

It was during this meeting that one member of the group stated that he had had the opportunity a few days earlier to meet with a Mayan priest from the Yucatan, who was visiting in the United States. The Mayan priest told him that he also had received information regarding the opening of the Egyptian portal and that it was scheduled to close on September 10th. (This information had come through independently from the messages that this group had received.) It was more than coincidental that the information should match so perfectly. Kuthumi had never given dates for the opening or closing of the portal; he only suggested general time frames for the group's departure.

But when Norma heard this, her heart sank. According to the itinerary that had been set for the tour they had selected and were confirmed to join, they were scheduled to be in the King's Chamber on September 11th, one day after the closing of the portal. To add to the dilemma, she and Rudy were scheduled to depart early the next morning. It was now 8:00 p.m. and there was no time to change the itinerary.

It was clear that the problem had been created when she and Rudy had interjected the three-day stay in Greece without consulting Kuthumi. Kuthumi had first stated that they were to spend seven days in England and nine in Egypt. If they had followed that itinerary, there would have been no problem. Since the itinerary had scheduled stopovers in Athens before entering and after leaving Egypt, it was clear that they should have planned to stay in Greece only at the end of the trip. The other problem was that Norma perhaps had not asked enough questions to get adequate information to prepare for the trip. The few times that she did ask for transmissions [the transmissions recorded in this book], Kuthumi only responded to the details that pertained to the major events of the journey. Everything else had already been taken care of with the travel agent.

Well, it was too late now. Feeling somewhat perplexed and defeated, they began their journey, hoping that all things were still in Divine order, but not really having faith that they were. How could they possibly get out of this dilemma? It seemed hopeless.

Needless to say, they never should have doubted the Masters. For one thing, everything occurred as the messages stated—with more ease and joy than could be imagined. The trips to England and Greece were spectacular. Coincidences sprang up continually. Connections with significant individuals were made that could not have been anticipated. It was hard even to imagine that a war was brewing so near, as the magic of the journey was so powerful.

The inner transformation that occurred in Greece for both Rudy and Norma was surprising, to say the least. Something was activated within their heads after they journeyed to Delphi. They each experienced a strange sensation within the third eye area, in which pictures, like slides, were flashed nonstop in their heads for as long as an hour. They could not shut off this phenomenon. It was not painful, nor was it annoying, but they could not control it. Pictures, in full color, flashed through their brains in fractions of seconds. Each was a complete image with a dialogue and a story, but the pictures were moving so fast that their conscious minds could not retain the information.

This happened to Norma when she was sleeping one night. She was awakened suddenly around 1:00 a.m. and experienced this phenomenon for approximately one hour before drifting back to sleep. The same thing happened to Rudy when he was on the plane flying from Athens to Cairo.

They experienced a different phenomenon on the way to the Parthenon. Suddenly, with no warning, as they were walking up the steps to this site, Norma had total recall of a past life in that area. She began to describe to Rudy the buildings, where they were positioned, the people, what they wore, their mannerisms, and the activities of the time. She did not know where this information was coming from, as she had done no prior reading on Greece before starting the trip. There had been no time to study. There had barely been enough time to bring through the few messages regarding the journey.

What was so fascinating about this experience is that the details she recalled all were verified by guides, friends, and the small museum that they toured later on the trip. The question was, from whom or where did all these facts and this knowledge come? Why did this phenomenon even occur? More importantly, what was the meaning of all of these occurrences and how did experiences like these relate to life and to "business as usual"?

The trip to Egypt was even more eventful. The group of five met at the Athens airport, boarded the plane, and headed for Cairo. They arrived at approximately 9:00 p.m. and hurried off to find their hotel. The itinerary for their tour stated that they were to spend two days in Cairo visiting the museum, shopping, and touring other sites. Then they were to take a plane to Aswan where they would board a riverboat and cruise up the Nile, stopping at selected temples along the way. After three days, they were to return by train from Luxor to Cairo, where they would visit Memphis and then the Great Pyramid of Giza. They then had two free days in Cairo on their own. That constituted the nine days in Egypt.

When they arrived at the hotel, it was nearly 11:00 p.m. No one was waiting for them because of the lateness of the hour. All the other members of the tour group had come in from New York together, but because of Kuthumi's schedule the five of them had made special arrangements to meet the tour group in Cairo. Therefore, they arrived too late to find out when they should join the larger group the next morning to tour the Cairo museum.

Before they left Albuquerque, the travel agent had told them to be prepared to be awakened early in the morning to go on the tours, for August and September were the hottest time of year in Egypt. Often the tour groups would get started early in the morning to avoid the scorching, dry heat of the midafternoon. So, the five of them were prepared for this. But because they had not begun the tour from New York with the rest of the group, and none of the five spoke the native language, they did not know the name of the tour group leader. Consequently, they did not know how to get information on the next day's activities. Therefore, they were forced to trust that all would be perfect.

They all were assigned rooms and went to them. They unpacked their suitcases, knowing that they would be there for two more days, and went to bed. At 3:00 a.m. they were awakened by an Egyptian steward knocking at the door and telling them to get up to begin the day. They remembered what the travel agent had told them about starting early, but this was absolutely ridiculous! With two hours of sleep, it was a little hard to swallow, having to get up in the middle of the night to see the museum. It seemed absurd.

31

Finally, two of the group members decided to go down to the lobby to see if they could get more information on what was happening. They were quickly informed that the river cruise boat that they had booked suddenly had developed engine trouble. The tour company was forced to combine their group with another, which meant that they were moved from a two-star cruise to a presidential four-star cruise (at no extra cost), and that the itinerary had suddenly been shifted. They were leaving for Aswan that morning, which explained the 3:00 a.m. wakeup knock. With this itinerary shift, it became evident that the five of them would be making their debut in the King's Chamber on September 10th.

Was there a doubt as to the Masters' power? The five of them stood there at 3:30 a.m. stunned, looked at each other, and just smiled. The level of movement, its swiftness, and its power were awesome. It tends to make one think, just who is in charge, anyway?

With this new information, the members of the group ran back to their rooms to repack, for they had approximately twenty minutes to get their things in order to start the journey. They mobilized quickly and were off to the Temple of Isis!

To describe all that occurred subsequently would require a novel. Events unfolded in a fashion similar to those described in this book. Day after day the group members were humbled, transformed, and awed by the coincidences and the synchronicity of events that occurred. There was no stress or threat, even though the threat of war was now being experienced near the borders of the country.

As always, each experienced everything on a personal level, and was guided to complete personal rituals, meditations, and prayers in selected sacred sites. The mission was completed on September 10th in the King's Chamber, and all was perfect. The group members went their separate ways, with Norma and Rudy heading home and the other three moving on to Greece and the Greek islands to complete their own itineraries.

On the way back to the United States, feeling very empowered that they actually had accepted the challenge to complete the journey, Norma and Rudy began to reminisce about their last few weeks and what the journey actually had meant. Rudy, in almost a flippant tone of voice, said, "Why don't you ask KH [Kuthumi] where he would like us to go next"? Taking out a piece of paper, Norma asked that question of Kuthumi. He replied:

Why not consider taking a journey to one of Earth's most powerful vortexes. We suggest the Bermuda Triangle.

Rudy and Norma just stared at each other. Shivers went up and down Norma's spine.

Thus, the explanation for this book....

---

[1]It is important for the reader to have some background information regarding the concept of the Templar in order to understand Kuthumi's reference, and why and how these messages connect. Therefore, a brief explanation follows.

In August of 1989, Norma Milanovich began to receive messages from Kuthumi on a structure to be built that would be a temple and a center for spiritual learning. The Ascended Masters named this structure "The Templar". Norma initially thought this would be a small center, to serve a local area. Additional messages from Kuthumi soon made it clear that this was to be a huge structure of great magnificence, which would serve all on Earth. It would be built in the shape of a pyramid, with a 500-foot-square base.

As further information came through, it became evident that this structure would have an impact of immense proportions on the world. One message gave the mission and five purposes of the structure. The message stated that this structure will:

1. be a tribute to God, the Creator of All;
2. be a tribute to humankind, and reflect the paths and accomplishments of humans throughout the ages;
3. be positioned as a stabilizing force for Earth to assure that the planet will not shift on its axis;
4. serve as an interdimensional communications center to allow Earth to communicate with other celestial bodies; and
5. serve as a transformation chamber to transform the physical bodies into Light bodies for all initiates who are ready to journey on to higher commands.

Since the initial messages, nearly one hundred transmissions have come through describing this structure in detail. The Templar will be built in the southwestern United States. In a message delivered to the United Nations Parapsychology Society in New York on October 3rd, 1991, Kuthumi stated that this structure is the rebuilt Solomon's Temple, which has been prophesied for centuries.

The scope of this project and its impact on the planet have required that an organization be established to support its construction. That organization is called the Trinity Foundation and is composed of a Council of Twelve. (For more information on this project, please see the informational page at the end of this book.)

The Templar is destined to be the subject of another book. Since it is not the subject of this book, only this brief explanation is provided here to help the reader see the connections to all the activities, projects, and transmissions that the Ascended Masters are spearheading.

[2] Codes (and keys) had been introduced previously in the Templar messages, so this concept was not foreign. It was not a surprise that the same approach was taken in the delivery of these messages. The messages that were transmitted later for the Bimini trip were all coded by Kuthumi for us to decipher.

[3] After these messages were received, and after the journey to England, Egypt, Greece, and Bimini, the Masters reaffirmed and sent through the precise alignments of the stars and constellations connecting the Templar with the heavens. What this message revealed is that we first had to journey physically to these locations to receive the programming and to activate the etheric records before this information could be sent through.

[4] If you, the reader, have travelled recently to Stonehenge, you are aware that the authorities have roped off the area, allowing tourists to approach the monument moving only counterclockwise. This confused Rudy and Norma at first, so they proceeded to walk around the monument as far as the path would permit, almost the entire circumference. Then they reversed the course and walked clockwise. The instant they did this, they both felt an energy shift in their bodies. The action created a distinct sensation, almost like a soft buzzing effect felt within their heart and solar plexus areas. It was powerful and real. This was interpreted as the alignment of the currents of energy that Kuthumi had talked about in his message.

For the reader who chooses to journey to Stonehenge, it is suggested that you might want to try this procedure, following Kuthumi's suggestions, to see if you experience the same sensation.

[5] It has been written that Jesus passed His final initiation in Egypt. When God said, "Out of Egypt I have called

my Son," some believe this means that Jesus assumed mastery after He passed his twelfth level of initiation and testing in the mystery schools of Egypt. The Great Pyramid of Giza is where all final initiations took place.

[6]While this message was being transmitted, a tremendous storm was occurring outside. Lightning was crackling everywhere, and sections of Albuquerque were temporarily flooded.

[7]Norma and Rudy had already planned a three-day stop in Greece between their visits to England and Egypt. In doing so, they had not consulted Kuthumi and were not aware that this action actually complicated the sequencing and timing of the trip. They were to find out later that it did, and were shocked to see just how swiftly the Masters were able to correct the problem that had been accidentally created.

PART TWO: THE VISION

Look well to this day...
For yesterday is but a dream, and
Tomorrow is only a vision.

But today well lived makes every yesterday
a dream of happiness and every tomorrow a
vision of hope.

Look well, therefore, to this day.

From The Sanskrit

CHAPTER II:
THE PLAN BEGINS

THOSE WHO went to Egypt were intrigued by the message Norma and Rudy received on the plane coming home—that the next trip could be to the Bermuda Triangle, to work in a powerful Atlantean vortex near Bimini.

Soon after returning home, a woman who had also gone to Egypt came to Norma for a private reading. At that session they asked questions about the proposed trip to Bimini. The answers received from Master Kuthumi contained the first details about the journey, and are reproduced below.

*...the trip is a reality if you **choose** to go. We would like to personally escort you to the highest energy point known to the beloved Terra, and request that you be accompanied by a group representing the Divine. We share the highest memory of that civilization and inform you that soon points in that Atlantean energy vortex will be reactivated for the planet.*

The ideal time for entering the portal is the second weekend in the month of February. This portal of time will be opened for only three weeks, and will open on the ninth of the month. It is advisable that your journey into the power spot coincide with the opening of this portal.

Soon, other souls of lesser vibration will be traveling to this location and will not be there with purpose.[1] This energy will weaken the connection. Thus, it is important to be there to access the energy before the others disturb the vibrations. It is in the vibrations that the encoding will occur. It is in the vortex that the scheduling of the programming will take place.

After we received these few details, the thought of participating in such a trip began to become a reality. Although the entire meaning of Master Kuthumi's words was not clear, it was evident that this trip was important, and one in which we wanted to take part. A phone call was made to a travel agent, and the plan was initiated. Soon after, through word of mouth, others felt drawn also to participate.

As we began to take action to make the trip a reality, a concern for many was the money needed to pay for it. A trip to the Bahamas sounded expensive, so we knew we had to create the belief that we would be supported in this adventure. All were aware of the laws of manifestation and the techniques needed to bring desires into reality. It seemed that making the commitment to the journey was a test of faith to:

1. allow the plan to unfold, and
2. trust that the financial means for each would be provided.

As each began to make his or her commitment, magical "coincidences" started to happen. The travel agent called to inform us that, for a limited time period, we could get a round trip air fare to Miami and back at two for the price of one—in other words, half price! This package was only available for travel to Miami, and just happened to occur when we were beginning to make our reservations. The package also stipulated travel to and from Miami at precisely the time we were asked to go.

One group member, who knew she was destined to make the journey, but did not have the money to pay for it, made a total commitment of faith and made reservations to go. When she told her employer and explained why she needed time off, he suddenly offered to pay for the trip in exchange for childsitting services at a later date. Not only did she get the time off, but her trip was fully paid for without going into debt! Another woman (who also did not have any funds, but made a commitment to go) shortly thereafter received a contract for work, which not only paid her bills, but also gave her enough money to go on the trip, debt-free! Several other similar incidents occurred, which gave many a means by which to pay their expenses. As these stories were shared among the group, there was a sense of wonder and a growing faith in the power of the Beings guiding us.

The woman who initiated the questions providing the first information about the trip was also concerned about finances. Yet, in spite of her financial situation and just previous to that session, she had made a decision to provide her healing services without charge to the many who would benefit from her work, but could not afford to pay. Knowing that this would make her own path even more difficult, she asked Kuthumi how she then might bring forth the money she needed for living expenses (and to go on this trip). The reply to her question was a beautiful analogy which we think deserves to be shared. It gives a common sense approach to the challenge of being on the spiritual path and still supporting life in the physical world. It is included here in hopes that it will be of benefit to any reader who has the same concerns in this area.

Blessed Child. Know that the message I am about to impart comes from the group of the ascended around the Tribunal Council.

We begin this dialogue with the study of furniture. Now, you wonder, why we begin with the study of furniture! I will tell you.

The Carpenter of the beloved Terra was one who understood the trade of exchange. He made, with His heart, the most beautiful of all crafts, and provided many with the gifts that came from His heart. He could do this because He was the one whom the world had given "the gifts of the Magi". This means He was able to provide to all, with only the charge of God's love, because He had passed all His initiations and could see with clear vision, will, determination, and LIGHT.

*If you possess clarity of these four qualities, then you also possess pure wisdom of manifestation and the gifts of the heart. If you have not passed the tests to the degree that the Carpenter has, then we suggest you begin work on your belief systems of the **will**.*

You possess all the characteristics of the Divine and of the Carpenter. You only do not believe this yet. If your belief system does not match your desires, then you cannot command the ability to manifest things to the degree that He did. Therefore, while your "training program" is in transition, may we suggest you request assistance from both worlds in your support and upkeep? Then, as you begin to increase your belief systems, and Divine will becomes stronger, you could slowly begin to drop the request for payment from the lower, third dimensional world, and move to the higher realms of the God Force.

YOU WILL ACCOMPLISH THIS FEAT IN A SHORTER TIME THAN YOU KNOW.

We suggest this transition to relieve you of stress that all children of Light do not need. Stress produces fears, apprehensions, and thoughts of the lower mind. In those thoughts also comes manifestation, for the universe allows you to reap what you sow. If you move to a point where you can bathe in Divine love, and still accommodate some expenses with the heart's request of payment for work well done, then you will alleviate some of the lower manifestations that you are sure to bring to you. Know that each creates his or her own reality by the thoughts each generates.

If you should heed this advice, you will move to the road of completion much sooner.

This is the collective voice of the Tribunal Council. You are free, as always, to follow any voice you choose. These are only our words of love sent to you this evening.

I close now, but send my peace and love to you this evening. Walk with assurance that all will be provided in the days to come. Learn of the inner calling to the wisdom of the ancients, and prepare well for an exciting journey back to Atlantis.

I AM Kuthumi, your Father and Guide in this millennium. Adonai.

Kuthumi's words told us that we must be practical and grounded in our work here on the physical plane. The message also suggested that we would soon see evidence of our growth and evolution in the manifestations that would occur. Indeed, the events which provided financial assistance for this trip showed many of us we were beginning to witness the demonstration of his promise.

There had been no formal promotion of this trip, but as word spread, the number of people who committed to take this journey continued to grow. Initially, we thought there would be just a few travelers. But as the weeks went by, the number grew to twenty, then thirty, until finally there were thirty-four who chose to meet destiny, participate in the adventure, and return to the lost continent of Atlantis to reclaim their heritage and help bring the world to the threshold of the Fifth Dimension.

In the following chapters, you will read the fifteen messages that Norma brought through to inform and guide us on this journey. We hope they will mystify, delight and intrigue you in the same way they did us. Perhaps they will even inspire you to make your own sacred journey to Atlantis.

---

[1] While on Bimini, we learned from the islanders that in the following weeks the island would be full of students from the mainland on spring breaks.

CHAPTER III:
THE AGENDA

NOVEMBER 11, 1990

KUTHUMI, I SURROUND MYSELF WITH LOVE AND
LIGHT AND REQUEST MORE INFORMATION RE-
GARDING THE AGENDA OF OUR JOURNEY TO
BIMINI.

*Good evening, Oh Daughter of the Command. I, Kuthumi,
welcome the opportunity to come through this evening to
provide you with further information regarding the upcoming journey in which you have agreed to participate.
We salute you, Rudy, Rudy Jr., and the others who will
soon make this event a reality. In your adventure you
will find many delightful moments for reclaiming the past
memories and keys that have led you to this present
moment of time/space.*

*The key to a successful journey to Bimini will be in your
abilities to access the Command's coding systems. What
I mean is that you will receive the symbolism that will
make your journey both intriguing and exciting. But
reality reveals that the intrigue will actually come from
your abilities to decode the keys. In the keys are contained the secrets to the power that Atlantis once knew.
This power was the connection of mind energy to the
source. It was harnessed energy of the sound frequencies,*

that must be combined with the color frequencies for manifestation to occur.

The key to the future for planet Earth is the harnessing of this energy, for when the decade of cleansing is complete, much that is around you today will have to be reborn. Therefore, one of the ways this will occur is to rediscover the paths and the keys of that former lifetime that will be used to rebuild the civilization as you visualize it to be.

The keys will be provided to you daily. The series of messages will be assigned each morning over five days. The messages will commence on Thursday and conclude on Monday of the following week. All individuals will receive their own coding to decode. Each must be attuned in his or her dual consciousness role, because each will be the receiver of his or her unique day's plan. Throughout each day's journey, each individual will be provided the clues to decode the signals that will be sent. At the conclusion of each day, the information that is needed to understand the solutions will be delivered. This will then have to be synthesized by each participant on the path.

We suggest that a discussion group be held at the conclusion of each day's session. The purpose would be to discover the keys and the codes that each was working on for that day's adventure. The members will be surprised at the similarities and the unified thinking that will occur at the end of each day, if they keep the silence of their day's journey until the evening hour discussion.

The parable of the fishermen who became frightened when the storm arose while Jesus was sleeping is appropriate at this point. If you recall, it was Jesus who silenced the storm when the disciples were awakened and forced to face their fears. I recall with much vivid recollection, for that moment was among my experiences.

Feelings of desperation may arise in some of the group when they relive moving into the vortex of Atlantis. It is necessary to relive this storm of emotion, for it will lighten the loads of the memories that each has carried for such a long period of time. Know that in the releasing of this memory, you will be freed to reclaim your mission and purpose for this lifetime. You have been prepared well in Egypt centuries ago, but have not experienced the trauma of physically moving into the vortex of the fatal scene that each of you knew so well. Move into this vortex once again, only this time you play the role of Jesus and calm the storm around with power from your Higher Selves.

A part of the journey is to help you reclaim who and what you are by facing the fear of this memory. Another part of the journey is to test your essence in earning rights to the power that was yours so long ago.

Information as powerful as what is scheduled to be released cannot be handed out freely to any casual observer who wishes to attend. The information must be received and earned on the inner levels. We advise that all be discussed in closed quarters at the end of each day.

The actual time for this journey need not be more than three days of physical presence on the island of Bimini. The coding will come in five, however, as we have mentioned. You may stay longer in that vortex, but we tell you with much assurance that it will be of no further benefit for the transactions that are destined to take place.

The island you land on could indeed be your place of residence. The North Island is actually a more ideal location for the proximity to one of the most powerful vortexes on planet Earth. We advise you take a journey onto the ocean and move thirty-five miles east into the vortex over the ocean. The structure that allows all time to stop is in this location. It is the presence of one of the most powerful crystal chambers on Earth today.

This crystal chamber, buried beneath the ocean floor, is scheduled to be opened from February 9th to the beginning of March. It will be seen in the etheric as the first step to anointing the chosen ones with waters and oils of the Christ. It contains the artifacts of the ancients and the vibrations of the Highest. It is one of the few vortexes that can withstand the seventh dimensional frequencies and unite them with those of Earth. It is here that we do much work. We activate many of the power centers on Earth through tunnels, such as this one, that provide us with such power.

These frequencies will be powerful and tranquil during this three-week period. It is predicted that the best time for your journey over this vortex will be Saturday, February 10th, or the numerical significance of the new beginning.[1]

Take these instructions seriously, for they will move your consciousness and the dream you will create on Earth. It will be in your renewed consciousness that each of you will be five steps closer to your goals and completion of your missions by the turn of this moment in history.

For the other days that you are there, contemplate counting the number of sands on the beach. Learn from the theory of the music of the spheres and find the perfection in the numbers. Take the turtle seriously and discover the coding in the symbolism of the back shell. Learn of their fight for survival as they continue to walk on shore through many difficulties and obstacles, to replant their seeds for the preservation of the species.

When you journey inward on this trip, know that the mysteries will be encoded within your cellular structures. The akashic records understand the decoding, and you need only match the two. Meditate with much discipline before your journey to prepare your mental states to withstand the tests that will befall you. Keep your centeredness at all times, and learn of the glory and Light of the Most Radiant One. This will be the key to your success in handling the intrigue and the destinies that will be yours.

I say no more at this time, but will provide you with more information in the weeks and months to come. Keep alert and move nightly with me to the Temple of Wisdom in the Great Central Sun. We will converse more intensely on an individual basis, should you choose to join us.

Good evening, Oh Daughter. Thank you for bringing this information through for yourself and the others. Now, please move to make your physical reservations, so that we may meet your move halfway with further etheric preparations for this event.

This journey holds many keys, as we said before. The true key cannot be underestimated.

I AM Kuthumi, your Father and Guide for this journey into the unknown. Adonai.

---

[1] In numerology, the 1 and 0 in the number 10 add up to 1—the number which implies new beginnings or cycles.

CHAPTER IV:
THE TIME/SPACE LESSON

NOVEMBER 18, 1990

Shortly after the November 11th message came through, Norma distributed copies to a few group members who had decided to go on the trip. Two of the group's members called her a week later to state that they were studying the message and had discovered that the Saturday Kuthumi reported to be February 10th was actually February 9th. Convinced she had finally caught Kuthumi in error, she marched over to the computer and entered this question.

KUTHUMI, PLEASE CLARIFY WHAT HAPPENED IN THE TRANSMISSION ON BIMINI. THE MESSAGE READS THAT FEBRUARY 10TH IS A SATURDAY, BUT IT IS A SUNDAY ON THE CALENDAR. DID I RECEIVE THE INFORMATION INCORRECTLY, OR DID YOU MAKE A MISTAKE?

Dearest Daughter in the Light of Our Most Radiant One. I, Kuthumi, come through this channel tonight to answer your question, for it is indeed important that we provide you with an explanation. To begin, neither is incorrect— you nor us—and both are correct—the date and day. Let us explain.

In the etheric, the dates and times are not as you see them to be. In linear consciousness there are methods for determining events based upon a frequency that you have labeled "time". This mode of operation allows for the event to be magnified in the instant in which it is occurring, but in reality, the event has already existed and will exist again at any given moment of time. Does this confuse you?

We will explain in another way. Take the momentum of a grasshopper. When this critter is leaping forward in time, the physical distance (space) covered during the leap can be measured. This means that the distance covered between the physical location of where it began and where it ended can also be measured through a time continuum, as well as through space. That is so for third dimensional reality.

In higher dimensions, all time is in the present moment of time / space. This means that any event appears in all points of the continuum and you can change or alter destiny in any way you choose. That is because of the lack of restrictions in perceptions one holds in the Fifth Dimension and higher.

When we presented the day of Saturday with the calendar date of Sunday, please remember that we also had said that the location which you were directed to is a place where "all time stops". What we meant is that the day of the new beginning of your journey would be the day of the ten. But because this location brings you to the intersection where the seventh and third dimensional realities meet, it was through symbolism that we represented that all time had stopped. You will travel on the 10th, to the day called Saturday, which has already stopped in this dimension. You will learn how to relive the keys and codes of Atlantis. This example of how they could actually control time is only one of them. By representation we gave you an example of just one thing you will learn.

Good night in the Light of the Most Radiant One. I AM Kuthumi. Adonai.

Norma's comment: "At times I feel like I play the role of the coyote in the roadrunner and coyote cartoon show. I would dearly love to 'trap' Kuthumi sometime. What an ego trip that would be! But somehow he always out-smarts me."

CHAPTER V:
WE COME FROM THE ETHERS AND
JOURNEY TO THE STARS

NOVEMBER 20, 1990

KUTHUMI, I SURROUND MYSELF WITH LOVE AND
LIGHT AND REQUEST ANOTHER TRANSMISSION ON
THE TRIP TO BIMINI. PLEASE PROVIDE US WITH
THE NEXT PIECE OF INFORMATION.

*Greetings, Daughter of the Command. It is I, Kuthumi,
again here to answer your need for further information
regarding this most important journey to Bimini.*

*"We come from the ethers and journey to the stars"
is the next piece of information important for you to have.
This message has encoded within it the vibration of the
ancients. It contains the keys to the unknown, and must
be unlocked before you can journey any further. Contemplate the message for the understanding that resonates
with your akashic record memory banks. Learn how to
unlock all, by using this as the example of how to move
frequencies from our level through you to the Third Dimension. Know that the understanding will bring great
relief and knowingness which will add to the confidence
each of you will gain from this experience.*

*The second piece of information important to know is
that each of you is divine. In that divinity comes the*

connection to all power in this universe, but not necessarily to all other universes. That is a quest we will introduce at a later time. In your own divinity you have the right to understand The All and command the right to rule the forces that operate in harmony with divine will. This understanding will be even more pronounced by the time you ready yourselves to take the steps into the vortex of Atlantis.

For you, Rudy, and Rudy Jr., we add another note—that it is desirable for you to leave the island of Bimini on your Tuesday, for reasons that we choose not to address at this time.[1] You will also arrive early to open the vortex for the group through the midnight ceremony that is scheduled to commence when the moon and the sun join in the celebration of the duality.[2]

We will provide many surprises to you on this quest, just like the travel arrangements that were readjusted. Believe with your hearts, and the mind of God will be joined within your third eyes to allow the ray of the dimensions to pierce your reality and world. Meditate seriously and surround yourselves with blue Light at all times. Archangel Michael will guide your efforts with instruction to teach detachment from the third dimensional reality. Let go of all that binds you emotionally and feel only lightness and love.

I AM Kuthumi, your Guide and dutiful Father for the day. Adonai.

---

[1] In a later session, Norma asked Kuthumi for clarification on why it was important for them to leave Bimini on Tuesday. She was informed it was because many personal agenda items would need to be handled quickly at that time to accommodate future events. Upon her return from Bimini, the activity was indeed hectic, and

suddenly resulted in Rudy's company repositioning him in Omaha and Norma having to make several important business trips to the east coast.

[2] This line was taken to mean that an important sacred ceremony would occur at sunrise on February 9th.

CHAPTER VI:
WE MOVE FROM THE STARS TO THE
INNERMOST PLANES OF CONSCIOUSNESS

NOVEMBER 27, 1990

KUTHUMI, PLEASE COME THROUGH THIS EVENING AND PROVIDE US WITH THE NEXT PIECE OF INFORMATION ON THE TRIP TO BIMINI.

Greetings, Daughter of the Command. I thank you for coming to the computer once again to receive the new directive. This piece of information will, no doubt, intrigue those who intend to journey to the sacred island.

"We move from the stars to the innermost planes of consciousness." That is the next piece of information you must have. Allow us to transmit our form of poetry too, which is the directive that accompanies our introduction.

> *We see with the mind's eye*
> *And glisten like the crystalline,*
> *When we observe the Light bodies*
> *Adapt to the chrystholen.*

> *The universe has no boundaries.*
> *The lakes have no form.*
> *The animals have no idols.*
> *And all humans are torn.*

SACRED JOURNEY TO ATLANTIS

The chrystholen will renew
All life and its forms,
Children of Light will be reborn
And the Earth will be adorned.

So, hasten to Bimini,
Come one and come all,
Move into the chrystholen,
And reclaim the Hall.

Justice will be served,
The night draws to an end.
Move with confidence and courage,
To your journey's end.

You have waited so long
For this moment to come.
Lead the way, Oh Children,
The stars wait for some.

Know truth will be revealed
In the days to come.
See justice fulfilled,
As the plan will be done.

Walk in Light and Peace, Oh Dear Children of God.

The above transmission verifies and defends the reason
why we requested you to journey to Bimini. Contemplate
the words and know that the message contained within
reveals the rationale for the journey. See the Light in
your minds' eyes as you read the statements, and use your
innermost wisdom and vision to help decipher the mean-
ing.

The second bit of information helpful for you to have is
that the location thirty-five miles east of Bimini is a point

of power over a section of water and Earth that contains a fifth dimensional beam which acts like a laser light to the higher dimensions. This point causes all time to stop, as it registers all vibrational frequencies of the different dimensions into the present moment of time. By passing over this spot, each of you will be activating your Light bodies and their subatomic structures, which will assist each of you to move into the Light dimensions for your missions.

This point of power is also the ray by which much symbolism is transmitted and decoded on Earth. It is the point where the Atlantean High Priests used their knowledge and powers to penetrate the crystalline structures and communicate with the Space Beings who were one with them in that civilization.

This practice has been lost to Earthlings, but will soon be reactivated by those who can access the frequencies and focus their mental energies to regain this information. The reason this is important is because it is one of the first steps to regaining the lost information of Atlantis that gave souls their power to transcend time/space.

Contemplate this message, Oh Commanders, and assume your positions to be wise students in the dream state.

I close this channel this evening. Walk with confidence in the days to come and learn through your inner avenues of knowledge. Adonai, My Beloved. I AM Kuthumi.

KUTHUMI, PLEASE DEFINE CHRYSTHOLEN BEFORE YOU DEPART.

Chrystholen means the golden Light that remains in the universe at all times. It implies the language of the Highest and demands the greatest discipline to learn. Only the Ancient of the Ancients who earned the highest positions in the civilization of Atlantis learned this scripture and its power.

CHAPTER VII:
INTERDIMENSIONAL PROTOCOL

DECEMBER 1, 1990

KUTHUMI, PLEASE COME THROUGH THIS MORN-
ING AND TRANSMIT THE NEXT MESSAGE REGARD-
ING OUR TRIP TO BIMINI. I ASK FOR PROTECTION
IN THE LIGHT AND THAT I RECEIVE A CLEAR CON-
NECTION AND READING.

*Dearest Daughter in the Light. Thank you once again for
your dedication to this assignment and for this opportunity to bring through another important piece of information for the Command. The next step of your journey
must include the instruction on protocol.*

*By protocol, we mean the set of rules and formal behav-
iors governing a meeting or encounter of dignitaries. For
a trip as important as the one to Bimini, there are certain
steps that should be followed in both the preparation for
the visit and the encounter of Beings interdimensionally.
To address this topic, allow me to change the frequency to
another dignitary, with whom you have never before communicated, and let this Master begin to prepare you for
the opportunities and tributes that will be yours.*

*The Master to whom I refer is called the Diplomat of the
Divine. He is the Being who guards the doors of the
openings to other dimensions and who instructs those*

*who wish to enter into the unknown how to do so. This
Being is called Delphor. He is the voice of the Sixth Dimension, and the one who guides many Starseeds home
when their journeys have ended on Earth.*

[There was a pause, and energy dramatically shifted
within and around Norma. Then, the following message
was transmitted.]

*Greetings, Oh Daughters and Sons of the Command. I
thank Master Kuthumi for this opportunity to meet you in
this manner and tell you we await your visit to our dimensional vortex, when you choose to move to the portal
over Atlantis. I have been asked to instruct on protocol,
a topic on which I am well versed.*

*The first instruction I will stress is that all come pre-
pared with the bath of the golden Light. This cleansing
must be accomplished, beginning three days before your
journey into this vortex. You should meditate on this
frequency and allow it to penetrate your essence. Know
that it is liquid and that this fluid will coat and protect
you as you begin the first moments of your journey.*

*Next, hold a clear conscience with your heart for every
single action, thought, or emotion that is within your
electronic circles. Allow everything of a disrupting vibrational nature to soar to the heavens to be recycled. Work
on this release, for it will be the releasing that will allow
you to be Light.*

*Next, see the vision with your inner eye of the impasse
Atlantis was experiencing moments before the fatal days
of the destruction. Try to measure the weight of the energies and to see how the imbalance of yin and yang
frequencies caused the world to shift the continents into
rebellion. If you practice the clearing as we suggested in*

phase two of this protocol process, then you will be free to receive this vision.

As Masters of Atlantis, know you can change the course of the world by focusing your own energies to create a new reality for the beloved Terra. See this new vision and the perfection that can be. Look with your inner mind, and see the ray of golden Light coming from your essence. Focus this light for thirty days before the 9th of February and direct its fluid essence to a point thirty-five miles east of the island called Bimini. In your essence will be the perfection of the plan being transmitted from your Higher Selves and the blueprints contained within. If you should be clear, your vision will not send a distorted message, and the coding and decoding will be in alignment. Use this force daily for a minimum of five minutes. This is critical for the perfection of the plan.

When you arrive on the island, give thanks to the Creator of the All for permission to return. Know that your souls have journeyed long and far for this opportunity to once again regain the status you had on that continent of so many centuries ago. You have been selected to go because of your essence. You have earned the right to lead the way again.

Each day, as you receive the first rays of sunshine around and on your eyes, know that in this vortex your eyes will allow the rays' energies to connect with the golden stream within your essence. Find this feeling of connectedness and oneness, and visit the sight of the ancients. Believe the voices within and hear the choir of the angels that will guide you. See the butterfly move your webs and carry the strands to the entire world.

When you are in this area, you will be directly connected with all major power points on the planet. The portal's opening guarantees that the energies of your essences will penetrate all points. Know that every thought you generate will be magnified through each of those power points a millionfold. Therefore, watch the protocol of your own behaviors and assure your Higher Selves that your egos will not rule for one minute on this journey.

The time of three days in this physical location will seal the messages that you have been directing to this point. Know that your Higher Selves carry the perfect blueprints for the future. Journeying there physically assures the stabilization of this imprinting, and the number three seals the perfection of the plan.

I will guide you through the doors and the portals. I will carry the torch of liberty to light your way for the future. You will be totally protected and guided every step of your journey. This is so!

I turn this communication back to Master Kuthumi, and await the next opportunity to address this distinguished group. Thank you my Sisters and Brothers of the stars. I AM Delphor.

This communication is now complete. I, Kuthumi, close this next set of instructions and seal them with the same procedures as we used in Atlantis. I take the number seven and imprint its power over these directions. The Lords of the Seven Rays of the White Light shall be entrusted to assure the perfection of the plan. This information will be taken to the vaults of the great library chamber in the Great Central Sun. The safekeeping of this information shall be sealed for seven months, at which time it shall surface again to heal the world of the wounds inflicted upon it by the fall of Atlantis. Soon that karma will be completed. With your help, Oh Dear Ones, it shall be concluded within this next solar year.

SACRED JOURNEY TO ATLANTIS

I AM Kuthumi, your Father and Guide. I instruct you in your next directive on the wisdom of the tunnels.

Adonai, My Beloved.

CHAPTER VIII:
SEARCH FOR THE HOLY GRAIL

DECEMBER 4, 1990

KUTHUMI, I SURROUND MYSELF WITH LOVE AND
LIGHT AND ASK THAT I RECEIVE A PURE TRANS-
MISSION THIS EVENING. PLEASE GIVE ME ADDI-
TIONAL INFORMATION REGARDING OUR UPCOM-
ING TRIP TO BIMINI.

*Good evening, Daughter of the Command. I come to you
to present the next piece of information you will need for
your journey to Bimini. I begin this evening with a salute
to all the Commanders who have elected to join us in this
powerful vortex, and to send you our gracious words of
gratitude and love. We promise you an eventful trip, and
one which will certainly bring your consciousness to heightened awareness. Now, let me begin the next message of
importance.*

*The chalice is the receptacle of the Holy Blood. In the
days of the search for the Grail, this cup was sought by
all the royalty and dedicated spiritual warriors who were
present on the Earth during that time period. Even those
who were not in physical search sought its essence on the
inner realms of reality. This is so.*

*In the days of Atlantis, this cup of truth held the symbol-
ism of the energy that unites with the physical body to*

sustain its higher consciousness and enlightenment. In the days of Egypt, this cup was delivered to the deceased in the afterlife, to assure that the ascensions would be fulfilled. In the days of Christ, the energy within this cup was held in the etheric until the appropriate time when all planetary alignments would be perfect and would support the physical ascension of the Most Radiant One.

For the group that is destined to journey to Atlantis, we advise that you once again become the spiritual warriors of long ago, and go to Bimini in search of the Grail. Find the cup and drink of its essence. Know that you will be privileged to drink from the container and become one with the elixir again. This search is only one of the reasons why you have elected to make this journey. This fact is only one of the reasons why you have taken it upon yourselves to serve the Most Radiant One.

To find the cup with the precious elixir, go north and then to the Fountain of Life. Move with the etheric and the stars. See Polaris shine down upon the Earth from a new position in the heavens. Look to Polaris for guidance in the New Age, for it is this star that will guide all to the Holy Grail once again.

This concludes the message of seven. Its power also comes from the dedication to the subject of this evening's message, along with the dedication to the Command.

Go in peace, My Beloved. I AM Kuthumi, your Tour Guide on this passage into the unknown. You are truly spiritual warriors. Adonai.

CHAPTER IX:
POLARIS AND THE MIDNIGHT CEREMONY

DECEMBER 5, 1990

KUTHUMI, FILL THIS ROOM WITH PROTECTIVE
WHITE LIGHT AND SURROUND ME WITH YOUR
LOVE. I NOW ASK YOU TO SEND ME ANOTHER
TRANSMISSION REGARDING THE TRIP TO BIMINI.

*Good morning, Bright Star. I come again to this meet-
ing room to bring more tidings of great joy to you and
the others who are making this journey. This message will detail that of last evening, when I presented the
idea of allowing Polaris, heaven's pointer, to lead the
way.*

*Polaris has been, and always will be, a significant way-
station for the Command. It guides all cosmic travelers
to their destinies and realigns the heavens' elliptical paths
every turn of the millennium. This star is so potent and
it radiates Light of such magnitude that it is the passage-
way between two universes. It is likened to a doorway, so
to speak, between parallel worlds. It governs the regula-
tory currents in this period, which will allow or disallow
the Earth to shift on its access.[1] Its power comes from the
Ancient of the Ancients, and its radiance guides all today
who are on a dedicated mission to save the Earth and
bring it into its glory in the years to come.*

SACRED JOURNEY TO ATLANTIS

Polaris gives strength and commitment to all who ask to receive its energy. It provides the strength of mental discipline, and when combined with the energy of Mighty Mercury, no-thing[2] can be stopped from completing its mission or destiny on Earth. We cannot stress enough the power of this star, for it is that which guides and rules even our course of destiny. Polaris is the way-shower for the masses into the New Age. It will provide the illumination that all children of God need to see their own divinity in the years to come.

Allow the energies of Polaris to direct your inner thoughts and ask that your minds be expanded to receive the quickness, alertness, and adeptness of Mighty Mercury. Move the currents of both these magnificent creations to your own inner consciousness during the next two months, and meditate on the brilliance that most assuredly will be yours in your own mental expansion.

Bimini is situated on Earth in a location where it receives the greatest amount of energy from Polaris, especially during this time of year. Therefore, know that you will receive a shower of brilliance during your stay on this island. A ceremony of the awakening of this energy to its full intensity is scheduled to commence at midnight on February 8th. This ceremony will include all conscious, sentient Beings who wish to participate in its offerings. To be on the island of power, during the power ceremony, to open up the most powerful vortex on Earth, says much for your obedience and dedication to your missions and the Command.

We say no more. Contemplate and design your futures, Oh Dear Ones, for the future will be yours. I AM Kuthumi. Adonai.

---

[1]The group believes this spelling was deliberate.

[2] The hyphenation of this word was deliberately inserted by Kuthumi. We believe it expresses an expanded meaning of the words "nothing" and "no thing".

CHAPTER X:
THE GAP IS WIDENING

DECEMBER 6, 1990

KUTHUMI, I SURROUND MYSELF WITH LOVE AND
LIGHT AND ASK THAT YOU TRANSMIT THE NEXT
MESSAGE REGARDING OUR TRIP TO BIMINI.

*Good evening, Daughter of the Command. Once again I
come through this frequency to address the comments that
must be read by the members of the group. The trip to
Bimini will be exciting and eventful. We will guarantee
that reality. One of the reasons why it will be so is
because of the electromagnetic energy that will be alive
during your visit to this sacred island. The currents of
energy will blow from north to south and will carry with
them the dreams of the elementals. They will have fire in
their veins, and will know that the time has come for the
reunification of the yin and yang energies on the planet.
Consider the time to be likened to the currents that will
embrace you. Your electrical systems will be altered by
the fumes of the forces that will be stirred during this
three-week period.*

*We see that not all of the group are taking these messages
seriously. We acknowledge those who are, for it is they
who will sail to the heights of the revolution after the
tides have shifted and the morning sun has dawned. We
address all with courtesy and respect and say unto all*

that we would like to work with each in a closer connection after the trip has been completed. The reality is that we will only be able to work with those who have raised their vibratory frequencies five digits, for in our path of evolution, so are we evolving and being consumed by the Great Central Sun. Therefore, as we widen the gap between our energies, we can and will communicate only with those who are maintaining their course of dedication and instruction. We say this not to alarm, but only to forecast the reality of what is. We wish for all to journey to our home and be our guests, but the gap is widening and we cannot control the course of the precession of the equinoxes. Know we address and love all, but will be able to touch the essence of only a few after the portal has closed on Earth. This is all a part of the process of the ascension. So be it.

Therefore, know there are three messages of importance within these words to help you decode the keys. Read with your heart and with your hands. This is the way to the higher realms.

Again I close this communication, but welcome the next session as we intend to demonstrate in a small way that which will be yours after the days of Atlantis.

I AM Kuthumi. Adonai.

CHAPTER XI:
JOURNEY TO THE VORTEX

DECEMBER 27, 1990

KUTHUMI, I RESPECTFULLY REQUEST THAT I BE ALLOWED TO RECEIVE THE TENTH TRANSMISSION REGARDING OUR TRIP TO BIMINI. PLEASE COME THROUGH AT THIS TIME.

Good morning, Oh Daughter of the Command. Again it is I, Kuthumi, hearing your request. I thank you for your attention to this most important matter. We wish to acknowledge your sense of urgency in completing the delivery of these last messages for the group. Please note that the final five transmissions are of short duration. Therefore, delivery of them will be expedient.

This transmission contains instructions for the journey aboard the ship that will take you to the power point over the tunnels of Atlantis. We advise extreme caution to those who wish to journey into the waters, for the currents are not what one would expect them to be in the calmer waters of Lemuria.[1] There is still turmoil in these areas, for the remembrances of the final days run deep within the consciousness of the Earth. Therefore, the ones who journey into these depths should know that only those with the highest of skills should take this journey, for the waters run to the depths of the unknown where the tunnels and openings to the hidden dimensions and worlds are located. We tell no souls what to do with their lives, but we look with great skepticism at the ability levels of those who wish to journey into this area, for the degree of safety does not support the degree of intent and dedication that we see emanating from their essences.

Once aboard the ship, take the journey with much laughter and delight. This will ease the inner pressures of the soul, as you move into the vortex of power. Know that in the moment of arrival, each will sense the fears and joys of the others, for this will be a moment of transference of power among the group members. See the Light from above in your inner eyes, and feel the presence of the moment. If you feel comfortable with this agenda, take a brief moment and conduct a meditation when you become still over the power vortex that you all once controlled. See that your inner and outer signs are balanced. This will assure two things: (1) that your female and male energies are balanced, and (2) that your yin and yang energies are also. This will provide a cross-stabilization of the energies, and will begin the harmonizing patterns for your destinies and missions.

There is nothing more you need consider for this part of the journey. We will do the rest, with your permission, of course. Know that any soul who is not comfortable with this agenda or any part of it should not consider participating. That is a given with no punishment attached. So be it!

I close now with this instruction and direction, but look forward to the next transmission, when Delphor will continue with the last information on protocol. Once again, we inform you of our love and dedication to protect each of you on your daily missions.

Goodbye, Dear One. I AM Kuthumi. Adonai.

[1]This was a personal message to a few group members who planned to go scuba diving in the area thirty-five miles east of Bimini.

CHAPTER XII:
THE VOICE OF TRUTH

DECEMBER 26, 1990

KUTHUMI, I SURROUND MYSELF WITH LOVE AND
LIGHT AND REQUEST YOU SEND THROUGH THE
ELEVENTH TRANSMISSION REGARDING OUR TRIP
TO BIMINI.

*Good evening, Daughter of the Command. Thank you for
returning to your computer once again to receive another
message of importance. It is I, Kuthumi, answering your
call for more information.*

*To begin, we send our warmest regards and brightest
thoughts of love to each of you who will be the recipients
of these words. We welcome your strength and commitment, especially during this seasonal change, and want
each to know that you are truly the fount of life for the
beloved Terra. Take these words as not only those of
appreciation, but also those of truth. For it is within your
essence that the elixir of wisdom and courage is held for
the entire world. The Christ energy during this time of
year is enhanced through giving. This energy comes from
the heart and is consumed with the power of the giving
and receiving that each soul experiences when celebrating
the birth of the Christ within. It is because of souls like
yourselves, who take the Christ energy to higher grounds
and allow us to use your essence in the transformation for*

the entire Earth, that we are able to make great strides in changing the vibrations on the planet. From our hearts to yours, may we say that you are beautiful and appreciated.

This introduction relates to this next message in two ways. One, the voice of truth rings in each of your souls, and therefore, you are the courage for the many who are now in embodiment on Earth.

Two, the voice of truth is what must be addressed in your journey to Bimini. This means that for each the journey will contain different truths. For those who are destined to receive the manifestation powers from the Higher Selves, truth means the living of the laws. For those who are destined to receive clearing, it means speaking the truth will make them lighter. For those who care not for the spiritual laws, but only for the moment of truth, it means they will ring of the magnitude of the present and will be grounded to a degree that they do not understand today. We say no more.

For those who understand the courage it takes to withstand the forces of souls who do not wish enlightenment to be anchored into the planet, they will see the justice of their efforts. The currents of the tunnels that hold the truths of the Grail will run deep within their veins, and allow them to understand enlightenment to a degree that they have not experienced before. They will know the color blue for the shields they will carry, and will also know that the nature of God is real and that it always has been and forever will be their shield. Courage takes on and needs no shield once the force of God is revealed and experienced. For the spiritual warriors who walk the paths of the Creator, courage is the code word for the decade of the nineties. These spiritual warriors are programmed for success. They need only look to their inner guidance, for they understand that the world is divided into mortals who see only separateness and illusion. For those who wish to separate the groups of the Earth into the original Tribes, they will experience success in their minds, and will feel heaviness in their hearts. Separateness breeds the pain of disillusionment and knows no limits, until the individual turns within and heals to become one within the Spirit. Look inward from now until the moment of your journey and feel the courage and truth that await.

Take the journey out onto the ocean floor with the courage and truth that all spiritual warriors understand. When you have arrived, know that in that location comes the moment of truth when you will be asked the question of your destiny. Take the moment to respond in the silence of your heart, and not with your mind. Feel within your heart the connection back to the star that gave you birth, and make the commitment to your ancestry that sustains and provides you with life. Know that the Creator of the All, the Mighty Great Central Sun, takes you to your maximum challenge in the curriculum of this day. Answer only with your heart as the question and challenge is put to you. In this moment of decision, each will experience lost time for a moment, which may not even be calculated in your Earth time and sequence of events. Only know that this period of silence will be present to rejuvenate your commitment to God and the Command.

The Brotherhood of the All welcomes you to the Order of Melchizedek's council table for debate. Hear the agenda before accepting the invitation, for acceptance requires that you are among those who can debate the issues on the table. The agenda items have been transmitted within these ten coded messages. Learn of the importance of discipline and move your consciousness to become one with the Highest.

There are simple laws for this membership. Always love God with every ounce of feeling that you have contained within your essence. Then learn to love yourself and others in a similar fashion, but always honoring the Father and Mother of the universe first. In this order come the code and the keys for successful passage into the chambers of the councils.

In conclusion, when one follows the Grail, then membership into the highest orders is assured. When one uses courage and truth to move to one's destiny, then the call for the question in the meeting will assuredly come. Once answered, the move to the membership will follow. When membership is secured, then know that active participation is required.

I say no more. There is little more to transmit, for all is given. Look to the inner Light for the coding and decoding, Oh Dear Ones. See your destinies unfold before your eyes.

Good night. I AM Kuthumi. Your Guide and Father for the journey. Namasté.

CHAPTER XIII:
DELPHOR'S FINAL PROTOCOL

DECEMBER 27, 1990

DELPHOR, I SURROUND MYSELF WITH LOVE AND
LIGHT AND REQUEST THAT WE RECEIVE ANOTHER
TRANSMISSION FROM YOU ON PROTOCOL. PLEASE
RESPOND TO MY REQUEST.

*Greetings, Oh Sister in the Light. Yes, I will be happy to
provide you with the instructions on protocol for the journey back to your island and homes.*

*The first thing that must be acknowledged, after complet-
ing your harmonizing pattern structures on board the
craft, is the expression of gratitude and thanks to
the Creator of the All. This can be done not only with
the heart, but also with the new color frequency that each
of you will experience. By visualizing this new frequency and giving it back in thanks to the Masters who
have so lovingly brought you to this point, you will be
allowed to move to the next level of initiation. As you
have probably surmised, the protocol on the higher dimensions of time/space is much more refined and digni-
fied. There is etiquette for obedience, for rulership, and
for membership on the Councils of the Most High. How
one enters and remains in these positions of power is to
follow the proper procedures of the heart and universal
laws. When this is done, the individual is then in*

harmony with the oneness and becomes a Being of eternal love and Light.

Take the hour of your return to the island and feel the earthy, stabilizing energies flow through your essence. Know that the direction from the northern to southern currents will change with your new polarization. The energies that will direct this new color and sound will now be polarized from east to west. In this crossing of the beams, you will be centered and fulfilled. In the fulfillment, you are ready to assume your missions of honor with the Command.

Protocol is nothing more than becoming one with the crossed energies of harmonization. Know that, if you turn all your attention to the outer self in learning to harmonize the inner truths and wisdom, you will be led to your destiny. This is a promise and one which will be kept.

Learn the curriculum well, Oh Children of the Stars. Know that your hearts will lead you to the refined positions of leadership in the future of which you all dream. Keep the bonds among the group and always use the strength of love emanating from the total population that will be journeying together on this memorable occasion.

In deepest respect and with the utmost of admiration, I now close this communication. I will not send another transmission to you before you take this journey into the Seventh Dimension. I only wait now to greet you on the doorstep of this memorable occasion. Keep the vigil burning in your hearts and look to your Higher Selves for all the direction and guidance you need.

I AM Delphor, the honored one who is pleased to have been called to assist you. Adonai.

CHAPTER XIV:
EL MORYA'S MESSAGE

DECEMBER 30, 1990

KUTHUMI, I ASK YOU TO BRING FORTH THE NEXT
TRANSMISSION AND THAT I BE PROTECTED IN THE
LIGHT TO ASSURE A CLEAR MESSAGE.

*Good morning, Daughter. I thank you for returning to
your computer to receive the next message from the Command. It is at this time that I, Kuthumi, would like to
turn the frequency over to El Morya, who will guide the
days of your journey to Bimini. As you have already been
prepared for this transfer of guidance,[1] I know you will
wish to hear his words of advice for the upcoming adventure upon which you and the others will embark. Please
stay in a centered state of being for the frequency to change
to receive the words of my friend and colleague.*

*Good day to you, our Distinguished Colleague. It is I, El
Morya, dedicating this moment to provide additional keys
and codes for the journey of this winter. My message is
short and contains three keys for your contemplation.
Therefore, study each word and know that in the energy
of each lies the opening to the sixth dimensional frequency
and higher.*

*The laws governing the vortex that will be opened over
Bimini are complex, but can be reduced to three. They*

are the following:

1. *Understand that north, south, east, and west are truly all one direction when it comes to the electromagnetic currents that rule the Earth.*

2. *Keep a perspective that balances the moon's energy with that of Polaris and you will reveal to yourself the secrets of the ages.*

3. *Believe that all power rests within your own consciousness, when ego has been eliminated.*

All of the universal laws are revealed in these three statements. The breath contains the depth of the knowledge and provides the means by which the third eye will open to reveal the understanding to each of you.

I thank you for this opportunity to speak to your group by this means today. My role, beginning February 7th, 1991, will be to assist each, who will allow it, to redeem the status he or she held in the civilization of Atlantis. These positions will be restored to those who seek them.

I AM El Morya. Peace be with you.

---

[1]This was a personal message to Norma. The day before receiving this message she had been told in a meditation that Master El Morya would be placed "in charge" of this journey.

CHAPTER XV:
KUTHUMI'S FINAL ADVICE

DECEMBER 30, 1990

KUTHUMI, THANK YOU FOR FACILITATING THE
TRANSMISSION FROM EL MORYA. I AM READY TO
RECEIVE THE NEXT MESSAGE NOW, IF YOU WILL
SEND IT THROUGH.

*Yes, I am happy to bring closure to this mission of the
Divine by providing you with the last two messages to
complete this series. Therefore, I will direct your attention to Part I first.*

PART I: ALIGNMENT

*As the group enters into the vortex that surrounds Bimini,
feel the currents of the wisdom that continually circulate
around the area. This moment will occur before the portal opens. In the days that follow, feel the currents of
wisdom shift. Know that in the shift will come your
alignment and harmonization which will bring you to the
threshold of the Sixth Dimension. When on that horizon,
you will experience the illusion of peace. But in your
physical reality, that feeling will be nothing but the exten-
sion of the energies of Atlantis that are projecting out-
ward to the universe to bring about a union between the
Earth and the higher worlds.*

Before you and the others take the trip, know that some may feel ill as their bodies are preparing for the ultimate of experiences thus far in their journey. Take this in stride, for the eight bodies attached to the physical existence will be producing an alchemic reaction in preparation for the journey. See this as a sign of completion and know intuitively you are on track for the event to be successful.

Prepare your minds well, and discipline yourselves for the thirty days before entry. There is no other way we can state with certainty and assurance that you will experience the ultimate, unless you take our words seriously. See with your inner eyes, and move your telepathic powers to the heights of new awareness. It is in this new heightened awareness that you will be guided to the planetary missions you are destined to fulfill in the years to come.

PART II: ONLY THE LIGHT GUIDES ALL OF OUR STEPS

This concludes the words we have prepared for your experience. Walk in the peace of the emissaries of the Divine. Feel the power contained within your cellular structures, and believe you are one with the Force. See your illumined bodies assume greater and greater responsibilities in the days to come, and see your own shadows of doubts and fears continue to fall away. The valleys of the shadows are no longer part of your landscape. They have served their purposes well for your emergence into the space in which you walk. Believe now that only the Light guides all of your steps, for it is in the Light that all will be revealed.

As we observe the passing of each initiation for all children of Light on planet Earth, we say with assurance that many pass the tests with higher vibrations than others. In the science of vibration comes the reunion of the Higher Selves with all that is within the physical worlds and consciousness of the individuals. Each of you who is dedicated to walk this path of illumination and to take this journey seriously is destined to walk with the Masters who have guided you so patiently all of these long years. Take their hand, for they are truly one. Then enter into the higher realms with the confidence that your Earth journey has been successful.

Go in peace and love, Dear Ones. I wait to meet you in the portal where all time stops. Journey with us and we shall direct your love and commitment to where it is most needed on beloved Terra today. See our ray touch each of you on your foreheads, throats, and heart centers. Then emit this same ray, which has been qualified by the hand of God, to each soul with whom you come in contact in the days ahead.

Step into the threshold now, that few have been permitted to enter.

Adonai. In the Light of Our Most Radiant One, I AM Kuthumi, speaking for the entire Tribunal Council of the Galactic Command.

PART THREE: THE EXPERIENCE

Some people look at things and say why.
I dream of things that never were and say
why not.

George Bernard Shaw

CHAPTER XVI:
INTERPRETING THE MESSAGES

By THE end of December, 1990, Norma had brought through the complete set of transmissions regarding the trip. By this time, two primary groups had formed that were planning to meet in Bimini—one in New Mexico and the other in New Jersey. Copies of the transmissions were sent to all group members who had committed to go. Both groups took the messages seriously and studied them at length. It quickly became apparent that input from the members of both groups was needed, and could greatly improve the ability to extract information and interpret the meanings encoded in the information.

When group meetings were held, either in New Mexico or New Jersey, opinions were presented on the significance of the messages. Some group members made notes of their opinions and shared them with others, in meetings or by mail.

There were several different ways the group members analyzed the fifteen messages. One method used was to extract all sections that pertained to direct assignments or instructions and to organize those into a separate file. That was a fairly easy, concrete thing to do. Others analyzed the content from a deeper, more symbolic level. This was a more challenging way to approach the messages. There was much speculation on the true meaning and symbolism of certain passages.

There was also a lot of significant general information given in the messages, as well as details regarding what we could expect to occur during the trip. Primarily, those details provided intrigue, causing speculation as to whether or not the events would actually occur. The individuals who exhibited greater confidence that those events would occur analyzed the passages and made predictions on how each event would actually manifest.

In this chapter, examples of the information extracted from the messages have been broken down into four categories:

1. Symbolism
2. Keys and Codes
3. Instructions for Third Dimensional Movements
4. Protocol, given by Master Delphor

In the pages that follow, an example of one group's effort to interpret the symbolism is given, as well as the Masters' interpretation of the same passage. In addition, selected pieces of information have been chosen as examples of each category listed above. We offer this information to give some possible guidelines as to what to look for when studying the messages.

Study and meditation on the messages is needed to grasp the true significance of the coded information. Much of the meaning can be interpreted on a personal level and may vary from person to person. Therefore, comparisons and group discussions are very helpful.

This chapter presented the most difficulty when writing this book, because of the undefined and mysterious nature of the information in the messages. Guidance from Kuthumi was requested on how we could organize this information for the reader. Kuthumi provided us with insight on how to represent the group's work in this book. The initial dialogue with him led to ideas of what we could do, such as defining important terms. His answers also inspired further questions. Some of that dialogue is printed below.

SHOULD WE PROVIDE AN IN-DEPTH EXPLANATION
OF OUR GROUP'S ANALYSES OF THE MESSAGES
FOR THE READERS OF THIS BOOK?

*We suggest not, for that amount of labor might rob them
of the ecstasy of discovering the answers on their own.
Since ultimate wisdom begins to unfold with the opening
of the third eye, and since this occurrence is associated
with higher level brain activation, we see that the readers
may be denied the opportunities to exercise their minds if
all interpretations are handed to them. Therefore, why
not provide examples of your work and know that that
will suffice in providing the stimulus for others to achieve?*

IN AN EARLIER COMMUNICATION YOU SUGGESTED
THAT WE DIVIDE THIS CHAPTER INTO FOUR SEC-
TIONS: SYMBOLISM, KEYS AND CODES, INSTRUC-
TIONS FOR THIRD DIMENSIONAL MOVEMENT, AND
PROTOCOL. WHY?

*The divisions were suggested to provide a framework upon
which to base an analysis. Challenging the reader to
interpret **Symbolism** provides an opportunity to stimulate the right-half brain structures, which dearly need
exercise. This will energize the brain and open up new
neural paths which will allow more learning and understanding to flow. A section on **Keys and Codes** enables
one to look at the smaller building blocks of information
that lead to the discovery of the ancient mysteries. An
analysis of the **Instructions in Third Dimensional
Movement** prepares the mind to move the body with the
proper agenda in the physical world. It also provides
readers with the necessary information to prepare for their
own journeys to the sacred island. Finally, a section on
Protocol could discipline minds and hearts to the sacred
rituals of respect, love, and obedience to God and the
laws. This section seals the interpretations with the*

reminder that discipline is the key to all paths entering the Fifth Kingdom and higher.

IS SYMBOLISM THE SAME AS THE KEYS AND CODES?

*The **language** of the universe is **symbolism**. Symbolism is that which directs energy into creation through sound vibration. Symbolism runs the world and all worlds contained in the universes of the macrocosm. The keys and codes unlock the mysteries of symbolism, enabling individuals to manipulate sound and Light frequencies through symbolic vibrations. Therefore, they—symbolism and the keys and codes—are one and the same. They only vary in the degree to which they are applied in your understanding. That is why you experience so much difficulty in trying to separate them in this document.*

Keys, codes, and symbolism are the categories individuals on Earth must learn before the trigger is activated to achieve mastery. Symbolism is the key to life and to understanding God. It is that which we are programmed to learn in our never-ending journey back to the Creator.

IN SPITE OF YOUR EXPLANATION, WE SEEM TO BE HAVING DIFFICULTY IN DECIDING WHICH ARE THE KEYS AND WHICH ARE THE CODES IN THE MESSAGES. PLEASE DEFINE KEYS AND CODES.

> ***Keys** — Small steps in learning that move one's consciousness from simple, linear concepts to more complex, higher ones. They are the tools that bring an understanding of the basic foundation for enlightenment.*

> ***Enlightenment** — The position achieved when an individual becomes one with the Higher Self and*

vibrates at the speed of Light. This new frequency prepares the individual to assume oneness with universal mind. This state implies one has access to all knowledge in the universe.

Codes — *Symbolic interpretations which require meditation to achieve the higher understanding. When one acquires enough of the basic steps (keys), one is prepared to manipulate that knowledge to assure that a higher understanding will come forth. Codes represent the symbolic form of wisdom that dictates to individuals the responsibility for interpreting the higher meaning. When one understands the codes, he or she has mastered decoding. When one decodes the mysteries, one becomes enlightened.*

WE HAVE SELECTED THE POEM THAT YOU WROTE AS AN EXAMPLE TO BE PLACED IN THE SECTION ON SYMBOLISM. IS THIS A GOOD EXAMPLE? IF SO, IS OUR INTERPRETATION CORRECT OR WILL IT SERVE TO MISLEAD THE READER?

The poem is an example of symbolism at its highest, for it not only contains keys and codes, but it also emits a vibration likened to the nectar that yogis describe when they have reached higher states of consciousness. The simple interpretation you provide is appropriate for display and will not serve to mislead the reader. Many who read this document will also interpret the meaning in a similar way.

If you feel comfortable in doing so, allow us to provide another interpretation, as well, to provide a contrast to that which represents the group mind. Doing so may serve to heighten the reader's awareness, if he or she will first anchor the thought that both interpretations are neither correct nor incorrect.

SACRED JOURNEY TO ATLANTIS

This last statement is provided to challenge students on the road to mastery, for I have just delivered another message full of deep symbolic meaning. Meditate on this too and see if this does not provide you comfort.

WE HAVE ONE FINAL QUESTION. WE BELIEVE THAT EVERYTHING WE PERCEIVE EXTERNAL TO OUR EXISTENCE IS A SYMBOL OF WHAT WE ARE EXPERIENCING ON THE INNER PLANES. IS THIS TRUE?

The inner planes govern direction and purpose for the journey. The world on the outside mirrors the reality that we create within. Every event experienced represents the truth of the journey encountered on the hidden dimensions of consciousness. Therefore, the mysteries each must learn to unfold on the inner planes are indeed the experiences acted out in the world around. When one understands symbolism, one is ready to move quickly and with grace in the world. This is truth.

Kuthumi's guidance was appreciated, informative, and helpful. The analysis presented below represents a small part of the group's attempt to pass the final exam for "Bimini 101". As you can see, it was not an easy task to study for this exam.

SYMBOLISM

The poem dictated by Kuthumi in his message of November 27th was one of the primary pieces of information worked on in trying to understand the Masters' symbolism. The following is one group's interpretation of this poem:

We see with the mind's eye
And glisten like the crytalline,

SACRED JOURNEY TO ATLANTIS

When we observe the Light bodies
Adapt to the chrystholen.

The Masters are joyful when they see our Light bodies begin to absorb the ancient, universal language, knowledge, and power contained in the golden Light. They observe us through inner eyes of wisdom and with a greater insight than we can imagine in our present form.

The universe has no boundaries.
The lakes have no form.
The animals have no idols.
And all humans are torn.

As the changes of the New Age come, all third dimensional beliefs and values are dissolved in the Light of transformation. This will create great turbulence and chaos on the planet, and in the collective human consciousness as it undergoes transformation.

The chrystholen will renew
All life and its forms,
Children of Light will be reborn
And the Earth will be adorned.

But the chrystholen (the golden Light containing the ancient language, knowledge, and power that our Light bodies are now absorbing) will regenerate all life on the planet. Certain individuals will be transformed into fifth dimensional Beings.

So, hasten to Bimini,
Come one and come all,
Move into the chrystholen,
And reclaim the Hall.

SACRED JOURNEY TO ATLANTIS

Come to Bimini, experience the vortex of Atlantis, regain the knowledge and power in the chrystholen that was once known, and reclaim the Hall. This could possibly be the Hall of Shamballa, or perhaps they are referring to an actual physical structure of Atlantis, which the Masters are using as a symbolic representation of the power we once knew.

Justice will be served,
The night draws to an end.
Move with confidence and courage,
To your journey's end.

Imbalances in the Earth's electromagnetic field, caused by the destruction of Atlantis that created so much negativity, will be neutralized, as will the effects of that negativity on us. We have earned the opportunity to reclaim the powers and privileges that were lost to us at that time.

You have waited so long
For this moment to come.
Lead the way, Oh Children,
The stars wait for some.

We have waited thousands of years for this opportunity, both to serve and to reclaim our inheritance. We lead the way for the children of Light, and some will achieve enlightenment and return to their star homes.

Know truth will be revealed
In the days to come.
See justice fulfilled,
As the plan will be done.

Walk in Light and Peace, Oh Dear Children of God.

The truth of the powers of Atlantis will be revealed in the coming times; and divine order, balance, peace, and harmony will be restored to our beloved planet Earth.

KUTHUMI, JEAN AND I HAVE DISCUSSED YOUR OFFER OF PROVIDING ANOTHER INTERPRETATION TO THIS POEM. PLEASE TRANSMIT ONE TO SHARE WITH THE READER. [Below is an explanation that Master Kuthumi sent through in approximately five minutes.]

The Ascended realms look on from above and watch the children of Light complete their journeys to the Fifth Dimension. The programming for total transformation will come when the DNA and RNA patterns within are decoded by the union with the Higher Selves. As the Higher Self enters the physical bodies, a new electromagnetic vortex of energy will embrace the other eight bodies contained within and around the individual. This explosion of energy will activate the planet's entry into the Fifth Dimension, which will cause much upheaval to the Earth, if the change is too cataclysmic and abrupt. Individuals may experience confusion and doubts, but they will always reunite with their own source of power. This reunion will serve to stabilize their consciousness and provide a new awareness as to the nature of reality in this higher kingdom.

These higher Light souls will grace the world and provide the keys and codes to others. The information they will then impart will be necessary to free individuals from slavery and bondage. The children of Light will be acknowledged by all for the gifts they will bring to Earth.

The vortex in Bimini is likened to a time capsule which is activated to speed up this process. The sooner one journeys to this location, the quicker his or her own time capsule will be activated. Fear not the journey, and ask not for courage. Instead, walk with confidence and reclaim the mastery that you know is already yours. Mastery is the journey. Mastery is the ultimate achievement.

Consider that the soul's journey is hastened in this lifetime to be rejoined with the Ascended realms. This is a realization that has taken many lifetimes to complete. Only some of the children of Light will move through the portal before it closes in the etheric, because the choosing does not occur on this side of the portal. The choosing occurs in the heart and mind of each individual who walks the path of oneness and enlightenment. Many will not choose, although all are called.

The time is fast approaching for all children of Light to regain their mastery. In this mastery will come all knowingness and love. Justice will be fulfilled when the judgment is final. That means that the vibrational levels will be achieved in a twinkling of an eye that will catapult the Earth into the Fifth Dimension. When this instant in time occurs, the electron will be spinning at such a rate that all will be silenced in the heart. This moment of time will fulfill the prophecy, and the planet will be birthed into a star in the heavens.

When comparing the two interpretations it becomes clear that ours was indeed "simple", as Kuthumi had said. This suggested that deeper study and meditation could bring forth a more profound understanding of the symbolism in the messages. Nevertheless, it was the first attempt. Kuthumi said that neither interpretation (ours or the Masters') was correct or incorrect. The authors understood this to mean that there are different levels of truth, depending on the perspective from which the symbolism is viewed.

SACRED JOURNEY TO ATLANTIS

KEYS AND CODES

Interpreting the symbolism that actually explains the wisdom of the ancients is not easy. Following are some examples of what we consider to be the most significant keys and codes contained in the messages that assist in accomplishing this. For the passages listed, we offer no interpretation; we only list them for contemplation.

Message: 12/6, Paragraph 2

> *One of the reasons why it* [the trip to Bimini] *will be so* [exciting] *is because of the electromagnetic energy that will be alive during your visit to this sacred island. The currents of energy will blow from north to south and will carry with them the dreams of the elementals. They will have fire in their veins, and will know that the time has come for the reunification of the yin and yang energies on the planet.*

Message: 11/11, Paragraph 16

> *For the other days that you are there, contemplate counting the number of sands on the beach. Learn from the theory of the music of the spheres and find the perfection in the numbers. Take the turtle seriously and discover the coding in the symbolism of the back shell. Learn of their fight for survival as they continue to walk on shore through many difficulties and obstacles, to replant their seeds for the preservation of the species.*

Message: 11/20, Paragraph 3

> *"We come from the ethers and journey to the stars" is the next piece of information important for*

you to have. This message has encoded within it the vibration of the ancients. It contains the keys to the unknown, and must be unlocked before you can journey any further.

Message: 11/27, Paragraph 3

"We move from the stars to the innermost planes of consciousness."

Message: 12/30 [Master El Morya's Message]

My message is short and contains three keys for your contemplation. Therefore, study each word and know that in the energy of each lies the opening to the sixth dimensional frequency and higher.

The laws governing the vortex that will be opened over Bimini are complex, but can be reduced to three. They are the following:

1. Understand that north, south, east and west are truly all one direction when it comes to the electromagnetic currents that rule the Earth.

2. Keep a perspective that balances the moon's energy with that of Polaris and you will reveal to yourself the secrets of the ages.

3. Believe that all power rests within your own consciousness, when ego has been eliminated.

All of the universal laws are revealed in these three statements. The breath contains the depth of the knowledge and provides the means by which the third eye will open to reveal the understanding to each of you.

SACRED JOURNEY TO ATLANTIS

INSTRUCTIONS FOR
THIRD DIMENSIONAL MOVEMENT

In studying the messages to extract the instructions for third dimensional movements, group members arranged the instructions in several ways. Some grouped them by concepts, and others developed a chronological timetable of things to be done, e.g., before the trip, while on the island, when in the vortex, etc. These lists or agendas were developed in order to better follow the Masters' instructions.

The following is an example of just one way the group listed these instructions. Also given are the quotes from the messages that were the basis for this agenda.

Agenda

1. Each day, be attuned in dual consciousness and receive individual codes for the day's itinerary.

2. Take note of clues given during the day, and summarize the information to understand the solution.

3. Conduct a meeting at the end of the day to discuss the information received. Compare and share messages and insights, and notice the similarities among information.

Message: 11/11, Paragraph 5

All individuals will receive their own coding to decode. Each must be attuned in his or her dual consciousness role, because each will be the receiver of his or her unique day's plan. Throughout each day's journey, each individual will be provided the clues to decode the signals that will be sent. At the conclusion of each day, the information that is needed

*to understand the solutions will be delivered. This
will then have to be synthesized by each participant
on the path.*

Message: 11/11, Paragraph 6

*We suggest that a discussion group be held at the
conclusion of each day's session. The purpose would
be to discover the keys and the codes that each was
working on for that day's adventure. The members
will be surprised at the similarities and the unified
thinking that will occur at the end of each day, if
they keep the silence of their day's journey until the
evening hour discussion.*

MASTER DELPHOR'S PROTOCOL

In his messages of December 1st and December 27th,
Master Delphor, whom Kuthumi called the "Diplomat of
the Divine", gave instructions that were described as
protocol, to be observed in preparation for the journey as
well as during the journey.

Webster's Dictionary defines protocol as "a code of pre-
cedence in rank and status and correct procedure in
diplomatic exchange". One of the things we were told
was that the instructions would prepare us for an
interdimensional meeting between "dignitaries". It appeared that this meant a meeting would take place between the Ascended Masters and us. This caused some
excitement, and we wanted to be sure to follow the protocol.

In following these instructions, the group members used
the processes he described for meditation, and took note
of all attitudes and behaviors that would be important in
certain situations as well as throughout the trip. The
following are examples of Master Delphor's protocol:

Message: 12/1, Paragraph 7

> ...come prepared with the bath of the golden Light.
> This cleansing must be accomplished, beginning
> three days before your journey into this vortex. You
> should meditate on this frequency and allow it to
> penetrate your essence. Know that it is liquid and
> that this fluid will coat and protect you as you be-
> gin the first moments of your journey.

Message: 12/1, Paragraph 8

> ...hold a clear conscience with your heart for every
> single action, thought, or emotion that is within your
> electronic circles. Allow everything of a disrupting
> vibrational nature to soar to the heavens to be re-
> cycled. Work on this release, for it will be the
> releasing that will allow you to be Light.

Message: 12/1, Paragraph 13

> Know that every thought you generate will be mag-
> nified through each of those power points a
> millionfold. Therefore, watch the protocol of your
> own behaviors and assure your Higher Selves that
> your egos will not rule for one minute on this jour-
> ney.

The four categories of information we have discussed
in this chapter are all important in preparing for this
journey. It is in studying the symbolism, however, that
the reader will find the most significant value of the messages. Therefore, in closing this chapter, we would like
to add these final words about symbolism.

We use symbols constantly in our daily lives. Symbols play an important role in the bridging of the thought world and the material world. The mind has a thought, and then creates an image or symbol that becomes the vehicle through which the thought manifests physically.

In just the same way that the mind can translate a thought into a physical manifestation, so can the mind translate from the physical back to the thought that gave birth to it, and also connect with the more expanded and profound concept from which it originated. All symbols hold a vibration which carry the essence of the original thought, and connect the symbol to the thought. Focusing on the symbol can, therefore, lead one to the original concept and also to the expanded awareness that surrounds the concept.

Words are symbols. Each word carries an energetic vibration. Different combinations of words carry different vibrations, which can be very powerful in their effects. Examples of these are mantras and affirmations, which not only create an uplifting effect on the individual using them, but also, when expressed with strong emotion and imbued with the power of the will, can set up the resonant field which attracts the energy necessary for manifestation to occur.

The point of focusing or meditating on the symbolism in these messages is to reach a state of expanded awareness which allows access to the truth and knowledge that is the higher essence of the symbol. One can then bring it to the conscious mind for use in deliberate creation. The ability to assimilate this higher knowledge for use is dependent upon the vibrational frequency one has attained within his or her own being, for understanding only comes when one is at a level of consciousness that can contain it. It is also true that study and meditation on the symbols can expand the consciousness and help raise the vibratory rate of the student, so that further expansion is possible and higher understanding is gained.

ΔACRED JOURNEY TO ATLANTIΔ

CHAPTER XVII:
THE BIMINI EXPERIENCE

IF ONE is fortunate, there are moments in life that stand out like shining jewels, shimmering and glowing long after the moment has passed.

Such a moment in time was the trip to Bimini made by thirty-four men and women in February, 1991. History may prove it to be a historic turning point for planet Earth. Much occurred during the days of February 7th through February 12th that not only affected Earth, but also imprinted the etheric. We will never forget those days in February, for we were told that we had the honor of being members of a group that performed a service for the planet. In return, each of us received gifts and blessings which have moved us all much further on the paths of our own evolution.

A group of near strangers came together to relive the tragedy of the destruction of Atlantis. Our journey brought the release of emotional blocks and fears caused by that trauma. We were told by the Ascended Masters that our presence in the Atlantean vortex assisted in cleansing the Earth of an energy imbalance created by the destruction, and gave us the opportunity to begin reclaiming the knowledge and powers we were told we once held in that great civilization, so that this understanding can be used to help heal the Earth and bring forth the Seventh Golden Age heralded for this planet.

SACRED JOURNEY TO ATLANTIS

Bimini

As the reader has already learned, the focus of our journey was the Bimini Islands. These islands lie approximately fifty miles east of Miami. There are two islands, North and South Bimini, which shelter a number of small cays and islets. The North and South Islands form a sort of horseshoe-shaped configuration, with a very small stretch of the Atlantic between them. The Biminis are part of the Grand Bahamas.

A quotation from *Edgar Cayce on Atlantis* tells us something about Bimini in relationship to Atlantis:

> *The position...the continent of Atlantis occupied is between the Gulf of Mexico on the one hand and the Mediterranean upon the other. Evidences of this lost civilization are to be found in the Pyrenees and Morocco, British Honduras, Yucatán and America. There are some protruding portions...that must have at one time or another been a portion of this great continent. The British West Indies, or the Bahamas, are a portion of same that may be seen in the present. If the geological survey would be made in some of these especially, or notably in Bimini and in the Gulf Stream through this vicinity, these may be even yet determined.*
>
> *The reading places the former continent or islands of Atlantis in the midst of the Atlantic ocean, as did Plato. It names the lands to which the inhabitants fled and the places where one might look today for evidence of this long-vanished civilization.* (pp. 52-53)

Bimini Magic

Bimini had a magic about it hard to describe. Perhaps it was because of the opening of the vortex, or the significance of the event that brought all of the thirty-four together in a bond that permeated the whole island.

The energy of the vortex caused many diverse personalities to come together and interact, with a sense of purpose in being members of this group. The energy also had the power to push all of our "buttons" over and over again, causing many spontaneous releasings and clearings. Instant relationships were formed that will never be forgotten, no matter how much time or distance comes between. The sense of unity and purpose felt among the thirty-four people was a rare and beautiful experience.

Time Warp

The day before we were to leave on our journey, one of the group members, a medical doctor, reported that in the morning, as he was writing a prescription, he checked his watch for the date. He noticed a very strange thing— his watch had begun to run on accelerated time. The date was advanced, and continued to advance throughout the trip until we left the vortex. It appeared that electromagnetic energies were creating a "time warp" and giving us notice of what was to take place in the vortex. Kuthumi had told us that controlling time was one of the powers held by the Atlanteans and that when we were in the vortex we would be in a place where time had stopped. The doctor's watch was a reminder that we were about to embark upon a journey which would be filled with intrigue and adventure on a grander scale than any we had known before.

SACRED JOURNEY TO ATLANTIS

The Beginning

The trip to Bimini will be exciting and eventful. We will guarantee that reality. [From Master Kuthumi's message of 12/6, Paragraph 2]

Our adventure began on Thursday, February 7th, 1991. In his messages, Kuthumi had told us that we would receive information for five days, beginning on Thursday, that would help us decode the keys to begin the process of regaining the Atlantean knowledge. As we gathered in airports, we all had a great sense of anticipation and excitement, and wondered what events would occur that would begin this process. As we were about to see, the adventure was truly going to be eventful. Some were to witness that the Masters were also not without a sense of humor.

Approximately half of the group arrived in Miami on Thursday evening, and stayed at a hotel near the airport. The next morning they drove to Port Wayne, and the tiny trailer that served as the terminal/customs office, to await the seaplane that would take them to Bimini. There was nothing around on this little finger of land. Suddenly, out of nowhere, a helicopter landed about forty yards from the trailer. As the travelers peered out the window, a man emerged from the helicopter wearing a Superman-like costume, complete with a cape, tights, boots, and a large "R" in the middle of his chest. Unable to contain their curiosity, a few ran over to investigate this "caped crusader" who seemed to have appeared for their benefit. When they approached, he loudly proclaimed *"I'm Mr. Recycle—remember to recycle!"* He then gave them the "thumbs up" sign and proceeded to walk around picking up trash and cans.

This incident reminded the group of a message from Master Delphor to:

SACRED JOURNEY TO ATLANTIS

*...hold a clear conscience with your heart for
every single action, thought, or emotion that is
within your electronic circles. Allow everything
of a disrupting vibrational nature to soar to the
heavens to be recycled.* [From Master Delphor's
message of 12/1, Paragraph 8]

The group members had a great laugh at this cosmic
joke reminding them of the message, and they were sure
that the Masters had set this one up just for their amuse-
ment. This event signaled an auspicious beginning for
this grand adventure, for "Mr. Recycle" reminded the
group of one of the most important keys to the whole
experience—to let anything disruptive return to its source
to be recycled, and to:

*Work on this release, for it will be the releasing
that will allow you to be Light.* [12/1, Paragraph 8]

With the memory of this lighthearted reminder fresh
in their minds, the first group of Atlantean travelers contemplated this humorous example of the Masters' symbolism as they boarded the plane to Bimini.

The first group arrived on the island around noon.
The rest of the travelers arrived in the late afternoon,
and proceeded by van and then ferry to the main street
of Alicetown, on the North Island, to find their motel and
connect with the first arrivals.

The group was divided between two motels on the main
street of Alicetown—the Compleat Angler, which faced
onto the street, and the Bluewater Inn, which was set up
on a hill slightly behind the other motel.

By 7:00 p.m., most of the group were eating dinner
together in the dining room of the Bluewater Inn, meeting each other and getting acquainted. That initial meeting was joyous. It was as if long lost friends had reunited

after a very long time. We knew we had been together before and were together again to renew our bonds, and to do the work we had promised to do. A sense of excitement surrounded all of us as we realized that we had finally come together to fulfill a common destiny.

The Wind

The weather was beautiful when the first group arrived on Bimini at midday on Friday. A mild breeze was blowing, and it was sunny and bright, not remarkable weather for that time of year. However, by the time the second group arrived, in the late afternoon, the breeze had become a very strong wind, and by evening it had grown to gale force, buffeting the palm trees crazily in all directions.

According to the islanders, gale force winds were unusual for that time of year. They commented on how strange the weather had turned. Our group instinctively knew that the high winds were due to the opening of the vortex foretold in Kuthumi's message. Filled with wonder, we tried to anticipate what would happen next. We were to see that this was just the beginning of a series of magical events that would bring home the truth of the Masters' messages.

The Opening Ceremony

Bimini is situated on Earth in a location where it receives the greatest amount of energy from Polaris, especially during this time of year. Therefore, know that you will receive a shower of brilliance during your stay on this island. A ceremony of the awakening of this energy to its full intensity is scheduled to commence at midnight on February 8th. This ceremony will include all conscious, sentient Beings who wish to participate in its offerings. [From Master Kuthumi's message of 12/5, Paragraph 6]

We met Friday night at about 10:30 p.m. so we could discuss the day's events, as the messages advised, and then hold the opening ceremony at midnight. It was an unforgettable evening. Outside, the wind continued to blow at gale force. Inside, the energy and excitement were growing. We talked about the messages we had gotten that day, and were amazed at how similar many of them were. We talked about plans for the rest of the trip and entertained each other with stories about our journeys thus far.

Finally, at midnight, we began our ceremony. We had set no agenda, but simply allowed events to unfold spontaneously. Three concentric circles were formed. We held hands or put our arms around each other, and the warmth of this connection spread through the whole group.

The ceremony lasted about forty-five minutes. Some were silent in meditative prayer, and others spoke of their thoughts and feelings of reverence and gratitude at being there. We joined in songs to celebrate Spirit and the Earth.

It was inspiring to take part in such a powerful ceremony. Some in the group saw, with their inner vision, a powerful column of energy come down into the middle of the inner circle and radiate out to encompass the whole room. The energy was electrifying and intense. Though we were not all aware of what had happened on a conscious level, clearly something important had taken place.

In his message of 12/5, Paragraph 6, Kuthumi had told us that:

> To be on the island of power, during the power ceremony, to open up the most powerful vortex on Earth, says much for your obedience and dedication to your missions and the Command.

We felt this honor and responsibility that night in the ceremony we performed, as we became one in purpose.

The Magenta Rose

Each day, as you receive the first rays of sunshine around and on your eyes, know that in this vortex your eyes will allow the rays' energies to connect with the golden stream within your essence. [From Master Delphor's message of 12/1, Paragraph 12]

...open the vortex for the group through the midnight ceremony that is scheduled to commence when the moon and the sun join in the celebration of the duality. [From Master Kuthumi's message of 11/20, Paragraph 5]

The next morning, many of us got up before 6:00 a.m. to honor Master Delphor's protocol and take part in a sunrise ceremony.

The morning was beautiful, though still very windy. We walked to different sites on the island, each person following his or her own guidance as to where they should be. Whether alone or with others, we silently experienced one of the most magnificent sunrises any of us had ever witnessed before. We sat in the stillness, allowing the rays to enter our eyes and connect with the inner Light. Slowly, a beautiful, brilliant magenta/rose-colored light began emanating from all around the sun, moving and swirling around the outside of it. The sky was flooded with a radiant gold that spread like a huge aura from the sun. Some saw the magenta light skip across the water to touch their feet. Others saw a silver blue light jump across the water. Some saw many colors around the sun, orange, coral, purple, green—a brilliant array, like a huge prism slowly rising over the water. The moon was hanging in the sky just above the horizon, very close to the sun. We witnessed this and remembered Kuthumi's reference of November 20th. Here before our eyes, was the evidence of the joining of the sun and moon, just as he had predicted.

We stood in silent prayer and meditation during the time of the sunrise. Peace and fulfillment came to us; we had received a great gift. We felt the wonder of those moments, as well as a profound sense of harmony. Each morning after the first, many rose early to experience the magnificent sunrise.

In Search of the Grail

> *To find the cup with the precious elixir, go north and then to the Fountain of Life. Move with the etheric and the stars. See Polaris shine down upon the Earth from a new position in the heavens. Look to Polaris for guidance in the New Age, for it is this star that will guide all to the Holy Grail once again.* [From Master Kuthumi's message of 12/4, Paragraph 6]

In this message, Kuthumi had directed us to go in search of the Holy Grail while on Bimini. The message appeared to be symbolic, yet, since we live in the physical world, it seemed appropriate to go on a physical search.

On Saturday afternoon, approximately twenty of the group members agreed to look for the Fountain of Life and seek the Holy Grail. We gathered together that afternoon in the stone courtyard of the hotel, and set off to the north.

The wind continued to blow, but it did not prevent the day from being warm and beautiful. We proceeded in a straggly line toward the north end of the island, taking our time and exploring along the way. We walked what seemed to be about two miles. Soon there was only a dirt road with just woods and brush on either side. We walked further and entered a section of the road that was sheltered by a line of tall trees. Everyone immediately sensed an energy shift—the area seemed to carry an intense vibration of stillness and peace. It felt like something that could, indeed, be called the Fountain of Life. The energy emanating from this area was intensely vibrant, soft, and radiant. It felt as if we were walking in a holy place.

To try to explain such a "vibration" is difficult—those readers who are sensitive to energies and who have visited high energy points on the planet will understand. It is a physical sensation of lightness and a sort of caressing feeling, and at the same time it affects consciousness by lifting one's spirits and increasing sensations of joy and peace. There is no mistaking this kind of energy shift— we all felt the change.

Two of the group were drawn irresistibly into the ocean, and emerged saying that it felt like "liquid love". Looking at the luminescent blue green of the ocean made one feel that this was the "color" of healing. In that special place, it seemed to radiate this quality doubly.

We spent quite a while just lingering there, exploring and enjoying this captivating area. Our search for the Holy Grail had led us to this experience of finding a place which seemed to radiate peaceful, healing energies, as a gift from the Earth.

The "Bimini Mack"

Some who had not gone on the outing had stayed behind to see about getting the boat that we needed to go into the vortex. Many of the group had been working on this intermittently since we first arrived. We had been advised by our travel agent not to try to secure a boat before arriving in Bimini. She felt that it would be easier simply to ask around when we got to the island. However, after some initial investigation, it appeared that there was not one boat currently available on the island that would hold all thirty-four of us.

When we arrived back at the hotel late in the afternoon, we found that there still had been no progress in acquiring a boat for the trip to the vortex the next morning, and it had begun to look as if we might have a problem. We had complete faith in the Masters' plan and in their ability to bring forth whatever was needed, and we had gone with our intuitive feelings that the boat would appear and we would be led to it. Now, as the time grew shorter, we wondered how the Masters were going to "pull off" this manifestation.

By 5:00 p.m., a small group of people sat in the courtyard of the Compleat Angler, which by now had become a central meeting place, and pondered the problem of the boat. Many had seen a large barge-type boat at the dock, with two main decks and a smaller top deck, which would have been perfect for the trip. Several inquiries had been made, all to no avail—it was the mail boat, called the "Bimini Mack", that traveled to Nassau and the other islands and that was, we were told, a federal boat—certainly not available for a "pleasure" cruise. Many said during the day, "That's the boat we need!", but all evidence indicated that there would be no opportunity for us to obtain it. Many other ideas had been explored, and none had been fruitful. There had been talk about the possibility of getting two or more boats, but no one wanted to split the group up, except as a last resort. On top of this, many islanders were saying that it was doubtful whether we would find someone willing to brave the extreme winds to take us on our journey.

Two of the group members, who were sisters, came back from shopping and joined the group in the courtyard. When they heard that we still had no boat, one of these women mentioned that she had seen a yacht she thought was big enough to hold all of us. The two sisters volunteered to go and try to find the owners of the yacht, to see if a deal could be negotiated.

They walked down to the yacht, which was anchored at a nearby dock, and spoke to a man who was standing near it. He told them that the yacht was already chartered for that weekend and was not available, but invited them over to his boat to discuss the matter. It soon became evident that the choices for a boat to take the group into the vortex were narrowing, if not non-existent.

Soon, this man's partner arrived and joined the conversation. They mulled it over and various ideas were discussed and abandoned. After a time of what appeared to be fruitless discussion, the two women were getting ready to leave, concerned about going back to tell the group that their attempt had been unsuccessful, when one of the men said, "Wait a minute! What about the mail boat?" An excited discussion about this possibility ensued, which ended with the two men giving the women directions to the local grocery store, where they would be directed to the house of one of the owners of the boat, who was also the captain.

At the grocery store, the clerk agreed to help them and pointed out the house, which turned out to be next door to the store and up a hill. As the two women approached the gate of the property, "coincidentally", the captain was just leaving. He met them at the gate, and they explained the situation to him. He said that he would discuss it with his partner and meet them where the boat was docked in just a little while.

The women hurried back to the other members of the group with their news, and several people made the short trek to where the boat was docked. There was much exclaiming over the fact that throughout the day various group members had commented that the mail boat was the perfect boat for the trip. The two women who had secured this connection had known nothing about the mail boat, nor that inquiries had been made about it and had been met with negative replies. It was apparent that they had been given the way and the path had been cleared for the group to get the boat through the "right" channels. The Masters' handiwork was evident to all, and it was exciting to trace the series of coincidences that led the group to the opportunity to obtain this vessel.

Several of the group met with the captain and his partner, and negotiations were completed. All details were finally settled, and a collective sigh of relief was breathed that the perfect boat, the only boat, had been delivered at the eleventh hour. It appeared that we had passed this particular test of faith and commitment, and were on our way to the vortex of Atlantis. Only one obstacle was left, and that was the wind. The captain had expressed concern that the force of the wind might stop us from making the trip, but we all went to bed that night knowing that the weather would cooperate and we would be able to make our long-awaited journey to the vortex.

The Trip to the Vortex

Sunday morning dawned clear and bright. Though still windy, it had calmed enough that we knew our trip was not in jeopardy. By 7:45 a.m. everyone was at the dock, waiting to board the "Bimini Mack". At 8:00 sharp we did our by now familiar countdown, to ensure that all thirty-four of us had made it, and then we all boarded the boat. The feeling of excitement and anticipation was intense among the group as we laughed and kidded each other. We were all eagerly awaiting the event that would take place over the vortex of Atlantis.

The captain and his crew of young island men were very courteous to us, and it was evident that we were quite a curiosity to them. In fact, we knew that most of the island people were very curious about what so many people were doing taking a boat out to the middle of nowhere. We did not want to fish, or to dive, but just to go thirty-five miles east and stand still for an hour. Some of the crew asked us what we were going to do out there when we stopped the boat. We did our best to explain, but it was clear that most of them did not really understand why so many had come from so far to do this strange thing. Even so, we shared a mutual enjoyment and companionship with the crew during the trip, and although they did not understand what we were doing, they seemed to respect our journey and understand that it was of a spiritual nature, and they were very kind and helpful to us.

There was a great deal of laughter and delight as we continued toward our destination. There were small groups all over the boat, which shifted and changed, with people leaving one and going to another, drifting from group to group and joining in the interconnectedness.

It is very difficult to put the feeling of this experience into words; to use the terms "love" and "joy" over and over only dilute the intensity and the tangible reality of the extremely intense energy surrounding the whole journey and the boat trip in particular. Thirty-four Atlantean souls had come together again after thousands of years to meet at the appointed place and time, to heal wounds— our own and those of the planet, to reclaim the mastery we had once known, and to receive our missions so that we might use the mastery for the healing and ascension of the Earth. We were told by the Ascended Masters that we would help correct a tragic and dangerous imbalance in the consciousness of the planet and of her children. We were also told that we would be rewarded for this work by being raised to a higher frequency, and by being given a gift chosen by the Higher Self. We would be part of an event that would create *"the highest vibration that has yet been recorded on the planet"*, and we were told that *"You have been selected to go because of your essence. You have earned the right to lead the way again"*. All of

these thoughts were in mind as we got closer and closer
to our destination.

During the voyage, many individuals and small groups
held their own meditations and prayers, invoking the
energies to empower and protect the journey and its purpose. The focus of our journey expressed differently for
each one of us. One of the group had received direction
that she was to be the "standard bearer and gate-keeper"
for the group, and to hold the energy to protect us and
our mission. She sat on the top deck meditating to hold
the energy for the full five hours of the trip, never waver-
ing. Her dedication and commitment were inspiring to
all of us.

Reliving the Destruction

*Feelings of desperation may arise in some of the
group when they relive moving into the vortex of
Atlantis.* [From Master Kuthumi's message of
11/11, Paragraph 8]

We had been advised by Kuthumi about this phenomenon, and as we drew closer to the vortex, some members
of the group began to have flashes of memory and to see
visions of their own experiences in Atlantis at the time of
its destruction. One of the group, who had never read
anything about Atlantis, had a sudden, intense vision of
the whole destruction. She experienced strong pains in
her head and her heart area, and began to sob as she
vividly relived the scene, and saw the decisions that had
led to the inevitable catastrophic result. She described it
as a sort of movie, one so fantastic that no Hollywood
producer could duplicate the effect. She described "destruction from the sky" by gargantuan lightning bolts,
and massive Earth movements that split the land and
made the whole continent shift and finally sink. She saw
the terror and heard the cries of people as they were

destroyed by this cataclysm. She described the chilling scene to many of us, and we began to gain a greater understanding of the incredible knowledge and power the Atlanteans had commanded, and felt with great intensity the consequences of their abuse of that power—of men and women believing, in their pride and arrogance, that they were the source of the power. In their ambition for power, they ignored their responsibility to God, to their brothers and sisters of Earth, and to all creation, and so brought death and destruction.

Many of the group had visions or experienced intense emotions of sadness, grief, and longing for a beloved home that no longer existed. Some gained the understanding that they had left Atlantis before the destruction, because they had known what would happen and could not make the leaders listen or change the course of their actions. These people experienced guilt and sadness, as well as a deep loneliness and longing for their brothers and sisters of Atlantis whom they had left behind as they escaped to new lands. One group member saw replayed the scene of her leaving for Egypt with her family to escape the destruction. Some, who had remained in Atlantis, also experienced intense feelings of guilt and responsibility because they had known what was going to happen and were unable to stop it.

The re-experiencing of these emotions was part of the reason we had traveled to the vortex of Atlantis, so that we might be free of this trauma, and reclaim the mastery we had lost in that experience—the powers that would enable us to fulfill our missions and play our parts in the plan to facilitate the healing and ascension of Earth.

The Love Zone

When we were about an hour from our destination, it seemed that we crossed an invisible line, into a new "zone", and that there was some sort of frequency change, creating a wonderful feeling of ease and peace. We began to talk about it, and soon most of the group had acknowledged that "something" had shifted; the energy surrounding us had lightened. We speculated on what the cause could be—perhaps the Masters had prepared this to help us with reliving our emotions from the destruction of Atlantis. It might have had something to do with energy being emitted from the crystal chamber that we have been told was under the water in the location of the vortex. Perhaps it was given to us so we could stay centered in order to face the question of our destiny that would be asked of us. We all felt this change, and knew we were nearing our destination.

The Vortex

As we approached the end of our journey, we saw in the near distance an unusual sort of mist or disturbance over the water. All around was totally clear, but there appeared to be a distortion of the air, a sort of haze of whirling energy over the section of water we were approaching. We grew excited, as we believed this to be the actual site of the vortex over which we were to stop. Muscle testing[1] was done by two of the group members and proved our anticipation to be correct. The place where we saw the mist was indeed where we were to stop the boat—it was the vortex we had traveled so far to find.

The DHL Boat

As we neared the mist, suddenly, appearing from out of nowhere, a small craft towing a rowboat and traveling at high speed crossed our path about one hundred yards away. We had not seen one other boat during the entire thirty-five miles of our trip, and this boat seemed truly to materialize out of thin air. One of the group recognized it as a DHL courier, which is an international messenger

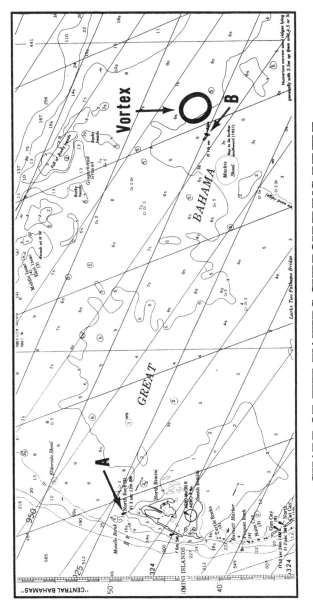

CHART OF THE WATERS SURROUNDING BIMINI

The arrow indicates the vortex thirty five miles east of Bimini.
"A" and "B" mark the navigation buoys that enable one to find the location.

service. Many wondered about the significance of this boat crossing our path just before we entered the vortex; we had long ago learned that everything in our outer lives is a symbol and has meaning beyond the surface appearance. However, our excitement at approaching the vortex quickly overrode our curiosity about the boat. As it turned out, we were not done with that boat, and later on it was to be the subject of much speculation.

The Meditation

At last our boat stopped, and all was silent as we looked around us. Amazingly, the water was very shallow, not more than twenty to thirty feet. It was the same beautiful, luminous blue-green color as the water around the island. The ocean floor was clearly visible, and covered with white sand. Many questions ran through our minds as to just what was really buried beneath that sand that made this such a powerful vortex.

We all climbed up to the top deck and sat in a circle. Then we closed our eyes and went into prayer and meditation.

> *Take the journey out onto the ocean floor with the courage and truth that all spiritual warriors understand. When you have arrived, know that in that location comes the moment of truth when you will be asked the question of your destiny. Take the moment to respond in the silence of your heart, and not with your mind. Feel within your heart the connection back to the star that gave you birth, and make the commitment to your ancestry that sustains and provides you with life. Know that the Creator of the All, the Mighty Great Central Sun, takes you to your maximum challenge in the curriculum of this day. Answer only with your heart, as the*

question and challenge is put to you. [From
Master Kuthumi's message of 12/27, Paragraph
7]

The Masters had prepared us well for this moment.
We had read the message over and over, telling us that
we would be asked the question of our destiny. Did we
commit ourselves fully to the service of God, and did we
accept our missions?

With these thoughts in mind, we meditated for about
forty-five minutes, until, one by one, we all gradually
returned in our consciousness to the top deck of this
Bahamian mail boat, thirty-five miles east of the Bimini
Islands. Many of us wondered just where our Higher
Selves had been, and what we had done in that time that
would dramatically alter the course of our lives, and perhaps the future of the planet. Had we been asked the
question, and how had we answered it? Did we all accept
our missions, and had we all received a five-step eleva-
tion in our frequency level? With whom did we connect,
and what information did we receive? These and other
questions ran through the minds of some of the group.
Others did not seem to be curious, but only accepted that
an event of great significance had taken place, and that
eventually we would know and understand all of it.
Several of the group actually appeared noticeably younger
and lighter, their faces glowing with an inner radiance.

Though we knew that we had received and channeled
energies as a group, the meditation had been a personal
experience for each member. Some shared their experiences. One person saw herself in front of the Tribunal
Council[2] being asked the question. Another group member saw all of us going up stairs in a line, taking our
turns to go before the Council. Others had visions of
what they had experienced in Atlantis. One saw her
Light body in a beautiful golden color, floating upwards,
and then saw golden and rose colored light pour down on

the group as they meditated. Another saw the face of a Master, who she believed was Jesus.

Many of the group did not speak of their experiences. For most, the asking and answering of the question did not occur on a conscious level, but appeared to be on the level of our Higher Selves, who spoke for us.

After all had "returned", we began to sing songs of Spirit and Light, some old favorites that everyone knew, and some new songs which we all followed along. Finally, we decided it was time to end the experience and head the boat back to Bimini. We began to descend to the lower decks, knowing one thing for sure—something important had happened, that would impact not only our lives, but also the destiny of the planet.

The captain was instructed to turn the boat around and head back, and we began the five-hour return trip to the islands.

As the boat started up, many expressed their thoughts that the trip would not be complete unless we saw dolphins; there had not been even a glimpse, as yet, of these graceful beings. Kuthumi had said that the dolphins are our extraterrestrial sisters and brothers, as are the whales, and some other animals on Earth. He said the dolphins have "hive" souls, which means that they are half human and half celestial. He also said that their radiance is so brilliant that if they had embodied in any other form they would have disintegrated. The waters of the ocean, like the fluid of the womb, protect and nurture them as they hold the Light for Earth.

Back to Bimini

The atmosphere among the group was much the same as before, but lighter and clearer, and a sense of accomplishment and purpose seemed to prevail among the thirty-four travelers. As we journeyed back to Bimini, much discussion took place, along with much laughter, and, for many, a feeling of euphoria that the long-awaited event had finally taken place.

About halfway through our return trip, several of us were talking to the captain at the front of the boat when we all saw a UFO in the near-distant sky make a broad swipe across the horizon and then vanish. There was no mistaking the shape and type of movement of the vehicle—this was no bird or airplane—this was the real thing. We wondered who it was, where they were from, and if they had "dropped in" to signal or salute us after our experience at the vortex.

The Dolphins

As we got closer and closer to our destination, many continued to express disappointment that we had not had a visitation from the dolphins. In fact, we had not seen one fish all day, even in the middle of the ocean.

The sun was setting, and we were about half an hour from the islands, when once again the DHL boat, still pulling the small rowboat, came from the left to cross our path again. This time, it came so close that it almost hit our boat, and the captain was forced to slow the boat nearly to a stop to avoid a collision. At the moment the DHL boat raced across our path, there were sudden excited shouts from the front lower deck—several of the group had been standing there and were the first to see eight or nine large dolphins leap into the air in front of the boat, and weave through the wake, seeming to signal a welcome return to the island after our great adventure in the vortex. Many felt the communication and connection with these wonderful Beings, and felt that their appearance signified the completion of our journey. The people in the DHL boat waved at us as they sped off, and we wondered again at the significance of this craft.

Immediately before the appearance of the dolphins, a few of the group had been below deck working with

Medicine Cards.[3] One of the group had pulled the dolphin and was meditating on this card when the dolphins appeared. He became known to the group, thereafter, as "The Dolphin Caller".

The dolphins also played another significant role in our journey. We had all noticed since our arrival that there were very few, if any, "tourists" other than ourselves on the island. The Ascended Masters were later to inform us of the part our dolphin friends played in this scenario.

Signals from the Sky

We were on our final approach to the bay. There had been a magnificent sunset, and we believed that our journey and the magic for the day had come to an end, when a large UFO was sighted, again near-distant, hanging in the sky and signalling to us with brightly colored flashing lights—red, yellow, green, blue, over and over. It was visible to the naked eye, though difficult to see clearly. One of our group members had a pair of binoculars, and through the powerful lenses the ship and the flashing lights were clearly and easily seen. There was much speculation as to whose ship it was, and who might be on it. It felt as if we were being greeted and welcomed back after our journey into the vortex, and perhaps also being congratulated on "a job well done".

I'm so Dizzy!

...take a brief moment and conduct a meditation at the moment when you become still over the power vortex that you all once controlled. See that your inner and outer signs are balanced. This will assure two things: (1) that your female and male energies are balanced, and (2) that your yin and yang energies are also. This

will provide a cross-stabilization of the energies, and will begin the harmonizing patterns for your destinies and missions. [From Master Kuthumi's message of 12/27, Paragraph 4]

Take the hour of your return to the island and feel the earthy, stabilizing energies flow through your essence. Know that the direction from the northern to southern currents will change with your new polarization. [From Master Delphor's message of 12/27, Paragraph 4]

By the time we arrived back from our trip, it was after 7:00 p.m., and the first thing on almost everyone's mind was dinner. We had all read Master Delphor's message many times over, but promptly forgot his advice to stabilize and ground our energies, and most of us went straight to eat. We had long since regained our "land legs", but most of the group began to experience dizziness and an inability to walk without lurching somewhat. It seemed as if something had been totally shifted in our energies, and we were having a very interesting time trying to accommodate the shift. This experience continued on and off for about two days, and longer for some. We definitely knew that we had been "repolarized" as promised in the message, and though somewhat uncomfortable, we were delighted with the physical confirmation of the change we had experienced.

The Sky Show

After our dinner and nightly meeting, the group members all went their own ways, assimilating the day's experiences. At about 10:30 p.m., two of the group members walked down to sit on the beach. Immediately they saw in the sky a large, light colored cloud that acted as a backdrop for five darker clouds which were in the exact shape of dolphins. They watched in amazement as the backdrop cloud began to change colors from a light pink to a deep orange. They tried to figure out where the light and color were coming from on this very dark night, and began to sense that something was behind the big cloud. They continued to watch in fascination as the dolphin clouds disappeared, one by one, and the big cloud changed into a long oval, and then to a circular shape, with five holes in the bottom. Through one hole, a beam of light came down over the water. The disk shape stayed for quite a while. Finally, at about 1:30 a.m., the "show" reached an end, and the two observers returned to their hotel, knowing that they had been a very fortunate audience for a deliberately choreographed spectacle in the sky.

More UFOs

In the very early hours of the morning, after everyone else had gone to bed, four hardy group members were still alert and awake. They had been sitting in one of the motel rooms, talking, when one of the group felt pulled to go outside to the beach, which was just yards from the room. All the group went out, and began to watch the sky.

Within moments, they saw several pinpoints of light in the sky. The movement of the lights was in a deliberate pattern that is typical of UFOs: moving at high rates of speed, suddenly stopping, zigzagging, disappearing and reappearing, moving up and then down, disappearing again, and generally putting on a show of movement that is only possible for extraterrestrial craft.

The lights began to change colors in response to the group's excitement, turning red, as if to match their emotion, then turning blue when they became calmer. The group felt a definite connection with the energies in the ships, as if these Beings were signalling to them, and making their friendly presence known.

The Fountain of Youth

On Monday, after a night of sleep to recover from the vortex, several of the group went on a tour of the South Island that included a stop at the Fountain of Youth.[4] In two vans, we took off to see the sights of Bimini. We saw the home of a former U.S. Congressman, and we visited a deserted resort on the tip of the South Island. There, our tour guides cut down fresh coconuts from the coconut palms and cut them open for us, or poked holes and put in straws so we could drink the sweet milk.

We pulled off the highway at a point that did not appear different from any other along the road, but our guides steered us to an opening in the tropical brush and we saw a much used path going into the trees.

The path turned, and just a little ways off the road, surrounded by trees, we saw a hole in the ground about two feet in diameter that went down about four or five feet. At the bottom, a little water was visible. With a bottle tied to a rope, one of our guides stood patiently bringing up water for us. During a trip to the site by a few group members on Saturday, one of the members had received guidance that we were not to drink the water, but to put it on the hands and wrists, the third eye, and the throat center. Most of us followed that guidance.

It seemed fitting that this fabled site was literally just a "hole in the ground" on an unmarked spot off the road, with no human-made enhancement or decoration—just the presence of the trees and the Earth and the warmth of the afternoon sun uniting in harmony to create a magical experience for us. There was a spontaneous desire to give thanks to the Earth for this gift; we formed a circle around the hole, linked arms, and sang a song of gratitude and praise to the Earth. We invited our guides to take part in this thanksgiving, and were surprised to have them do so with enthusiasm. As we loaded back up on the vans, there was a feeling of connection between these island men and our group that had not been present before.

The Last Night

That evening, we had our last dinner together. The group met at a small cafe on the main street of Alicetown that had prepared in advance for this crowd of thirty-four hungry "tourists". We enjoyed our dinners of seafood and various local delicacies as well as the camaraderie of our fellow interdimensional travelers. There was a sense of finishing, and an excited sense of beginning also, for we all knew that we would leave the next day to return to our respective worlds and begin to implement the missions we had received while in the vortex.

There was much laughter and "table-hopping" as we all discussed our various experiences. There was also a great deal of picture-taking and many heartfelt promises to keep in touch with each other. We knew, although such promises are always well-meant but often not kept, that this was one group of people who were irreversibly bonded in common purpose.

We had met each night, as Kuthumi had instructed us to do, to compare the information and guidance we had received, and were always surprised at the similarities among our messages. That final night we met once again, to share for the last time the perceptions we had received and the experiences we had had throughout the day as we pursued the paths on which we were guided. We also expressed our deep appreciation for one another, and for those Beings who had guided us so lovingly on this journey.

A special and beautiful closing ceremony had been prepared by some of the group members. We closed this final meeting with deep gratitude for the great adventure we had experienced and for the parts we had been chosen to play.

The Final Day

On Tuesday morning, many of us awoke for our last sunrise on Bimini, and were again entranced by the vivid colors blazing from the rising sun.

We proceeded to go about our final day's affairs; some left on the early morning plane, while others had until the late afternoon departure to shop for souvenirs, enjoy the beach, or relax in their rooms. Many of us felt reluctant to leave this scene of our grand adventure, and all of our new family whom we had grown to appreciate. Many vowed to return to the beautiful little island again to relive the wonderful memories of this journey.

We knew that something important and wonderful had occurred, to us and to our beautiful planet. Just how important and wonderful, we would not know until some weeks after returning home, when we received the message from the Ascended Masters that described the true significance of our journey. But that is another chapter, for you, the reader, to discover.

IMPRESSIONS

When we returned from our trip, a questionnaire was sent out to group members, asking each to write a brief description of his or her most memorable experience on the trip. The following are excerpts from some of their replies:

K.B.:

As we started into the vortex, I felt a deep, profound sadness. I did not know why, but sensed that

I was reliving some of the sadness of that past lifetime in Atlantis.

L.B.:

Prior to arriving at the vortex, I viewed my work
station in Atlantis, which was an energy station.
The apparatus that was used for energy generation
required a combination of sound and light along
with crystals.

Once we arrived and stopped the boat in the
vortex, I saw during the meditation an overhead
view of a large area that was destroyed. Nothing
was left standing. The rubble appeared to be
in blocks of material that had an adobe-like color
to them. As far as I could see, there was nothing but rubble. Some of the residue had distinct
shapes such as a corner piece or section of a doorway or a window frame. The hillsides were littered
with those blocks, while no buildings were left standing.

After viewing the destruction, I asked when I
was scheduled to travel to the Council to answer
the questions. The response that I received was
that the schedule was here and now and there was
no preparation time! The question that was posed
was, "What are you going to do differently this time
around?" I answered that it was imperative that
we use energy and energy systems for higher purposes and not as destructive implements. The response received indicated that energy and energy
systems were used for far more destructive purposes than the rubble that I observed. What made
the improper use of that power far worse was that
it was done with the knowledge of how physical
reality was but a mere fraction of the whole picture.
What followed was a dissertation on how energy
was improperly used.

Energy was used to control thought forms of individuals. Even though an entity may generate peace, love, and harmony, energy was used to block the manifestation of some forms. The universe accommodates all thought forms that are created as long as they are not blocked or inhibited. The blocking of free will in the terms of thought forms is indeed an atrocity. Our mission this time is to ensure that energy systems are used for the greater good. We must get more involved in the usage of such energy systems.

P.C.:

The initiation experience aboard the boat at the Atlantis vortex was the most memorable experience of the trip for me. The ceremony and meditation on top of the boat was incredibly powerful and infused with loving energy.

In my own meditation, I saw a group of us, all attired in white robes, standing in line and ascending a stairway to stand one by one before a Light-filled Being at a podium, with many other Light Beings in attendance. There was a discourse between this Being and each initiate; then many loving presences came to surround and accept the new one. After this event, we each went to stand around the perimeter of the room, a very large room with tremendous crystals around the edge, and we stood in front of the crystals. The ceiling was open to the blue sky and clouds. There was a solemn feeling to the occasion, like a graduation ceremony, also much joy and peace. I felt as though I had accomplished that which I had come to do. I had been graduated and accepted.

SACRED JOURNEY TO ATLANTIS

B.C.:

The most memorable experience for me personally was frequently seeing the new red-orange color when I closed my eyes. I first really saw it when we got to Bimini, but after the experience in the vortex, I could see it almost constantly. I assumed that it was the sun, or just the way it would be from then on, but indeed after leaving Bimini, I began to see it less and less often, and came to really know it was the energy of love.

J.C.:

One of the most memorable experiences was the insight into the yin/yang energy imbalance before the collapse of Atlantis, which I received during a sunrise meditation. I really felt the tremendous imbalance that existed then. My key experience was in the realization or recognition of how the yin force had to totally surrender to the yang experience. The "Sons of God", so to speak, saw the inevitable collapse and realized that, other than expressing their understanding and insight, resistance would intensify yang entrenchment in their position. And thus I could understand why many went out to establish new beachheads of wisdom and truth in other parts of the world.

L.C. (teenager):

The day after we went out to the vortex we were all together, it was so nice. In the morning I saw the sunrise. It was beautiful seeing the new colors that were formed. Next, my family and I rented scooters and went to both ends of the islands. At one end there was a forest with beautiful trees. It was really nice because we were all together.

SACRED JOURNEY TO ATLANTIS

T.C. (teenager):

My most memorable experience was finding the Fountain of Life. The whole group got together to find it. We knew basically where it was, so we headed in the general direction. It was a beautiful day in that the sun was bright and the sky a bright blue. The wind was fairly strong, creating a cooling effect which was excellent. Later we entered a more private area of the island and I noticed a change in energy. It had an uplifting, calming, and loving effect on me. What a feeling!

D.D.:

On the boat in the vortex we had all connected hands and lay in deep meditation....I was suddenly thrust into a remembrance of another time. Evidently, it was the memory of drowning during the last tragic days of the existence of Atlantis. I had been part of a ring of temple priestesses who had connected hands and, with a faith and dignity that was almost palpable in this vision, had descended into the ocean depths. I recalled vividly holding the warm, vital hands of the other priestesses until the currents finally swept us apart. As I was disconnected from the others, I was struck by the icy coldness of their hands as they succumbed to their watery graves. I re-experienced in that brief moment the helplessness and anguish of releasing my sisters, although I knew quite well that we had been prepared by initiation and training to confront this upheaval. My final flash of remembrance involved catching sight of a black, shadowy presence (a predatory creature—a shark), which overtook me. At that moment I experienced a sensation of terror mingled with resignation and surrender to my role in a great planetary energy shift and the demise of a legendary civilization.

SACRED JOURNEY TO ATLANTIS

M.G.:

On July 2nd, 1990, while on a trip to Cerro Rabón, Mexico, I had a dream that I was taken on a space ship. I was taken over the islands of Bimini and given many details about them, but specifically about the seven Atlantean pyramids that had been present in what is now a lagoon. I was told that I would visit the islands in the near future.

On the day following the visit to the vortex, February 10th, 1991, while sitting on the edge of the lagoon, I was shown the seven etheric pyramids.

My watch began to demonstrate accelerated time on February 6th, 1991. It registered forty-four days between February 6th, 1991, and February 10th, 1991. It stopped registering accelerated time as soon as we left the vortex on February 10th.

K.M.:

My most memorable experience on Bimini was the coming together with more of my spiritual family in total oneness. The total unity that was experienced was a miracle and a glimpse of what our future holds.

M.S.:

The most meaningful experience came when I returned home. I had brought back a conch shell found on the beach in Bimini. I placed the shell on my desk and forgot about it. One day I was near my desk and began to intuit something about the shell. Under the guidance of Ascended Master El Morya, I was guided to move the shell to a wide window sill where I have other things such as stones, crystals, and a six-inch pyramid, and to rearrange each object into an alignment that created a healing vortex in my home.

SACRED JOURNEY TO ATLANTIS

J.T.:

Our spiritual journey to Atlantis marked the culmination of many old spiritual connections and the beginning of the most remarkable new spiritual linkages for my own journey back to the Godhead.

The message I received, "No longer the cross, but the bee", was very personal. I have since dropped the "cross" of false friends...I have gained the honey or wisdom of many new worker bees in my life. Atlantis marked the end of the burden or guilt of the cross. It marks the beginning of the joy of cross-pollination from many new and exciting mutually supportive pathways, including stronger relationships to those who choose the future.

I no longer measure spiritual travelers by their outer path—mine included. I have learned to seek the honey, reject the falsehoods of the past, and enjoy the blossoming of new flowers or Starseeds.

J.W.:

Most memorable for me was the homogeneity of the group. When thirty-four people come together, there is usually some conflict or friction. But in this group, there was alignment on the goal to do our work in the vortex; therefore, there was no friction but only commonality. That was remarkable to me.

Also memorable to me was the experience of physical change after being in the vortex. The shift of polarities continued to cause physical sensations such as vertigo, headaches, and seasickness well into my return trip home. It was indeed an indication that the energy in the vortex is powerful.

---

[1]The testing was done by professional kinesiologists. Muscle response testing accesses information from the Higher Self, through the brain, and into the muscles being tested. In the above case, precision muscle testing

was used, isolating the anterior deltoid muscles in both arms. Both the tester and testee must be grounded and in balance to obtain accurate answers. This is checked by various techniques and corrected if necessary. In this process, the testee's arms are raised in a position in which only the anterior deltoid muscle is in action. The tester asks the question of the testee's Higher Self and then applies a gentle pressure to the arms. The testee's arms will stay strong if the answer is positive, and relax if the answers are negative. Yes and no answers were used to ascertain the location of the vortex, and then other codes were established so that the testee's arms would relax when the exact location of the vortex was reached.

[2] Tribunal Council refers to the Tribunal Council of the Galactic Command, which is the governing organization for this parsec of the universe. This group of Ascended Masters is responsible for administering and coordinating the plan designed to transition Earth into the Fifth Dimension.

[3] Medicine Cards: This refers to a set of beautifully illustrated cards and an accompanying book which comprise a divination method based on ancient tribal wisdom and teachings from the animal kingdom. *Medicine Cards: The Discovery of Power Through the Ways of Animals* was created by David Carson and Jamie Sams. Copyright 1988 by Bear & Company, Santa Fe, New Mexico.

[4] Fountain of Youth: A spring of legendary fame, which was said to have rejuvenative powers. It was sought in Florida and the Bahamas by many explorers, including Ponce de Leon.

CHAPTER XVIII:
THE BENEDICTION

FOLLOWING THE journey to Bimini, several group members wanted more information on the hidden significance of what transpired while we were there. Each had his or her own version, making the number of stories equal to the number of members who made the trip. After numerous sharing sessions and reports, several individuals suggested that we request a transmission from Kuthumi that described, from the Command's higher perspective, the events that unfolded. We decided to ask, and everyone anxiously waited to compare their versions with the "official document".

Two weeks after returning from the Bahamas, Norma sat down at her computer and asked the following question. The total response, however, was so long that it took three sessions at the computer to bring through the message as it is recorded here. The following is what the Masters transmitted.

FEBRUARY 24, 1991

KUTHUMI, I SURROUND MYSELF WITH GOLDEN LIGHT AND REQUEST PROTECTION TO RECEIVE A CLEAR TRANSMISSION FROM YOU THIS EVENING.

THE GROUP MEMBERS KNOW WHAT THEY EXPE-RIENCED BEFORE, DURING, AND AFTER THE JOUR-NEY TO BIMINI, BUT WE WOULD LIKE TO KNOW

SACRED JOURNEY TO ATLANTIS

WHAT "REALLY HAPPENED" ON THIS TRIP. PLEASE PROVIDE US WITH YOUR INTERPRETATION OF WHAT HAPPENED AND WHAT SIGNIFICANCE THIS TRIP HAS FOR OTHERS WHO MAY WISH TO MAKE THIS JOURNEY.

Dearest Daughter in the Light of Our Most Radiant One.

I, Kuthumi, come through this evening to provide answers to the questions you ask. We delight in explaining the significance of your journey to Atlantis. Please understand that this experience is just the beginning of your travels and enjoyment in the years to come.

Before I begin, allow me to turn the frequency over to the Diplomat of the Divine, Delphor, to assure that all protocol is addressed in this closing tribute to the group. Please stand by for an adjustment of the frequency.

[There was a long pause and the energies shifted. Then the following message was transmitted.]

Good evening, Sister and Delegate to the Council.

It is I, Delphor, addressing you and the others in this formal manner to assure that all etiquette is complete and the stage is set for closure to this memorable and historical event. I come to honor each of the group members, and to state that the Tribunal Council is, indeed, pleased with the work and the tribute that was made in respect to the request you fulfilled. The journey you undertook was a historical one for the beloved Terra, and will register on the etheric for eternity.

The members of the Council send their applause and commitment to each of you for your dedication and duty in working to bring in the highest vibration that has yet

138

been recorded on the planet. They state with assurance that you will be rewarded in the days to come for your personal sacrifices in choosing to take the journey into the unknown. The real work is yet to begin, and they affirm that the missions will soon be revealed.

With this introduction, I now return the frequency to Master Kuthumi, who will instruct you on the learning that took place in that vortex over Atlantis.

[There was another pause at this time, and Kuthumi returned to transmit the following message.]

I return, Oh Daughter, to fulfill your beginning request.

During the three-day period on the island of Bimini, the Earth shook and trembled in the etheric. The electromagnetic seas stormed the horizons and the anguish of the last days of Atlantis was relived. By Sunday, the period of intense pain had reached its climax. The rivers of the flooded waters overflowed with emotion and the remembrances of the final decisions that caused Atlantis to sink to its destiny.

Your group membership of thirty-four brought a new peace to this vortex as you sang the praise of God and quieted the turbulent seas. The energies there shifted, because of the energies of the individuals who participated in this event.

Each member who was called to return to this sacred point did so for a different purpose. All returned because they understood that this journey was significant for the beloved Terra. They intuitively knew that this was their mission. What each member was not so cognizant of was that each one was also reliving a personal journey from another dimension in time/space. It is in this reality that

139

we would like to focus this discourse to answer the question you originally posed to the Council.

If you recall, in the earlier messages we stated that all would receive individual programming on this journey, because the benefits and the experiences would be different for each group member. This is so! The reason there could be no set agenda that would encompass all of the group's needs was because, in the etheric, there are akashic remembrances for each individual that not only transcend time and space, but also mark the positioning of the blueprints for the future. Every member who journeyed to Atlantis is scheduled to fulfill a different mission in the years to come. All of the blueprints and programming for the missions are contained within the Higher Selves.

The Higher Self is, in actuality, a seventh dimensional energy vortex which you might call the Light Body. Since Light is Earth's curriculum, and the highest vibration known to humans, it is natural to understand that the Light Body is a seventh dimensional manifestation. When we requested you to focus your attention into the vortex for thirty days prior to your journey, and project the golden rays of your highest image for the future from your Higher Selves, you were actually participating in your own self-programming for the years to come. This action guaranteed that each of you would receive unique guidance from your own Higher Self, and not from an outside influence that might wish to distort your path.

So, as you entered this powerful vortex, the first thing that actually occurred is that you received your missions. That is why so much activity has bombarded your lives upon your return to the mainland. Or have you not noticed how everything has been moving with such rapid force in the last several weeks?

SACRED JOURNEY TO ATLANTIS

The second thing that occurred is that you all partici-
pated in learning and deciphering the codes. We ob-
served that some accomplished this activity with greater
ease, and we acknowledge the growth exhibited. This
new inner awareness will benefit each, because what was
learned will be directly connected to the individual mis-
sions in the future.

Learning is never enough unless one learns to apply the
results of knowledge. While in the vortex thirty-five miles
east of Bimini, each saw, in the etheric, his or her own
future and how to use the knowledge gained. While many
do not recall this today, we say that this is so. In the
years to come, this will become evident.

The levity that many experienced will also be a part of
this learning and application, for it will determine each
one's ability to handle pressures that will surely befall
you on your paths. The power of humor cannot be under-
estimated. It is this emotion that sings of the Divine,
when it is handled with good taste and respect. We ob-
served that many of the group brought this gift to the
journey and taught others to receive its gifts, as well. We
compliment all who used this skill to lighten the loads of
the others. In the years to come this vibration is certainly
destined to be one of the highest of them all.

Many times we are accused of not having a sense of
humor on this level of existence. This, we assure you,
is simply not so. We do understand the importance
and gravity of the plan, but we also know that the loads
we carry are lightened when we are able to reduce
anxiety, and the energies that cause energy blockages.
Therefore, we encourage you to develop this talent fur-
ther, and to provide others with instruction on the gift of
laughter.

SACRED JOURNEY TO ATLANTIS

The next event of great significance was that you held a communion with your sisters and brothers of Hydra as you watched the dolphins dance around your boat. They came at the end of your journey into the vortex to officially seal the energies of that day's events, and to bid you farewell from your visit to one of the most sacred places on your planet. The dolphins were with you every step of the way, and were actually protecting the island from other "intruders" to assure your privacy on the trip. That is why you did not see many other tourists on the island while your group was positioned there. Your sisters and brothers of the stars were emitting an official radar signal that prevented others from coming during the time reserved for your work. The dolphins understood their role and completed their work with great ease and dedication. They are delightful Beings to work with from this level, for they always approach any mission from a point of total love and Light. They were shining the Light all around the island for your privacy, and took their turn in the vortex to assure that your vibrations were anchored into the turbulent vortex over the power spot of Atlantis.

Atlantis actually went under the sea over 10,500 Earth years ago. The painful memories of the cries and the pleas for assistance have been in the etheric over that sacred spot for all of this time. Know that the Earth has tried to reposition itself for centuries to undo what it created in that critical moment, but has not been able to realign itself to accomplish this. There has never been a moment in history when the critical mass which actually commands the power to reset the course of action for the Earth to accomplish this has been as great as it is today. In the greater civilizations of the past, the populations were fewer in number so there were not enough souls to actually change the tide of events through the processes of their thoughts. Even in Egypt, where all the mysteries were known and mastered, the effects were only applied to those who commanded the knowledge and wisdom. This is because the currents of energy that were emitted from the few who understood were only strong enough to change the vibrations and course of destiny for that region of the world.

For the first time since Atlantis, there are finally enough souls in embodiment all around the globe to make a difference in changing the direction of the world. This is because the population is as large today as it was during the time of Atlantis and Lemuria. Many former Atlantean souls are incarnated again on Earth for the sole purpose of assuring the safe and easy passage of Earth into the Seventh Golden Age. These souls, who are positioned all around the planet, are uniting today to collectively change the vibrational patterns of the world. That is why so many are called frequently to the power vortexes and the precise ley and grid lines which ignite the positive energy flows into the Earth.

Each does his or her duty with the highest of regard and respect for the beloved Terra. These highly advanced souls are also old souls who intuitively know that they are one with the beloved Earth. They understand how they are one with the energies of the Divine, as well as understanding the connections we make within and between all that is. They are the ones who are sowing the seeds on the planet to assure that it will grow from a planet to a star, in the constellation of the Highest.

What the group of thirty-four accomplished in this regard was to affect all Starseeds on Earth by the magnification of the energies through this vortex at this time. You also brought the seventh dimensional frequencies through by acting as the electrolytic converters for Earth, and allowing these energies to be magnified through this vortex to affect every sacred power point on the planet. You shot the rays of the golden Light into the hearts of each star child, and focused the love, and its intensity, through your own Higher Selves to those who needed this energy to fulfill their own inner missions.

Therefore, you collectively worked to secure linkages with all the inhabitants on Earth who are working to make the paths of love and Light the way for all followers in the future. In your courage and leadership, three things were granted to each of you.

1. *In the future, you will automatically receive the programming of one of the three stations that were described in an earlier transmission. Your courses and destinies were set at the closing of the seventy-two hour period in Bimini, based upon the programming from your own efforts and commitments from your Higher Selves.[1]*

2. *Each of you was granted the gift of total freedom in the years to come. This is truly a gift, for not all on the planet are free of karmic debts. You will not experience the repercussions of actions in the future that are truly deemed by you to be for the highest good of all concerned, even if your discernment levels are not compatible with your choices. Your dedication has provided you with the freedom to work in service to humanity now, while at the same time receiving your further tests of initiation.*

3. *In speaking of initiations, each group member was automatically advanced to the seventh level or higher in accomplishing the steps toward his or her mission. After tests of commitment always come tests of power. For each soul who chose the path of the spiritual warrior, the new agenda means that life will automatically get easier and more fulfilling.*

Therefore, your personal journeys have guaranteed this gift, and the awakening from this point on will truly be more rewarding.

The strength that each is feeling in the heart center upon returning from this sacred journey is actually the result of all that has been explained thus far. It is a physical sensation which represents all that has been stated up to this point. In reality, this inner strength is actually something else, but will take a while to explain. Bear with me as I digress here momentarily to deliver a story of significance which will explain the point I am trying to make.

With your permission, I will now begin.

Journey with us to a moment and place in time where all live in oneness and dedication to God. Carry the torch of freedom with you on this journey, and allow it to light your path. This Light is the energy of your soul, and it takes the wise person to see that this Light is contained within all humans and other sentient beings who walk the path of enlightenment.

The place to which I escort you is Shamballa. This city in the etheric has been recognized by many mystics and scholars to be positioned over the Gobi Desert. The highest vibration known to Earth is in this location, and, therefore, many emanations of the Divine come to Earth from this position. Shamballa is the ideal for all who are striving for the love and Light within them to be realized. It is likened to the Holy Grail, and the essence of its attunement refines the soul on the path to the higher states of consciousness.

Higher consciousness guides the spiritual warriors in this New Age to conduct feats of courage. This state of mind is only realized when one's individual etheric bodies are aligned with the higher vibrations of Shamballa. To move to a point of higher consciousness automatically means that one enters the etheric city, and moves within this other dimensional frequency even while in embodiment on the Third Dimension of Earth.

This might sound confusing to the average reader, so allow me to elaborate further on the meaning of higher consciousness. When we use the expression "higher consciousness", we are actually referring to the intelligence one uses when the third eye is opened. The third eye holds the key to all states of higher abstraction and learning. In this experience, the initiate wanders in worlds that are new, exciting, and beyond normal description. When one actually has the gift of inner sight, then that individual understands the significance of Shamballa, for he or she journeys to this city by invitation and partakes of the elixirs that banish all thirst in the third dimensional existence.

The opening of the third eye brings total, lucid dreaming and awareness for those who choose the path of enlightenment. In experiencing the inner faculties and completing the work of the Masters, the individual learns how to integrate intuition with mind energy. It is in the reunion of these faculties that the individual becomes more confident in the decisions and manifestations that are actually happening. When confidence grows, so does the inner calm, for this is the time of greatest growth.

In the vortex over Atlantis, off the shores of Bimini, each of you received an awakening that caused your third eyes to be programmed with information for your individual missions. You became one with the Divine in a dimensional frequency that caused you to be more influenced by the vibrations of Shamballa than at any previous time in your lives. Because the vortex is connected to all main

146

power points on the planet, you were accessing a millionfold return on both your investments and the impact of energy on you. In this magnified electromagnetic field, you were actually accessing the power of your own Higher Selves, which were being prepared to assume their positions within your physical bodies.

The higher consciousness each of you received is what provides you with the inner strength and calmness you are now expressing. On one level it is likened to your own sense of security, because you are actually stronger and more secure being five steps closer to your own divinity. The experience in Bimini could bring you only five steps closer to your own totality of being, for anything beyond that, with such intensity, could harm you physically or mentally. When an individual walks the path of the spiritual warrior and mastery, the time it takes to achieve mastery is extended to years, for the path of transformation affects all nine bodies within one's essence. Therefore, five steps on an accelerated program is the maximum "voltage" that any individual can take at any given time, to assure safety while on the path.

Usually individuals also need rest for approximately sixty days following an event such as the one you experienced. Knowing this, be prepared again to receive more acceleration in the month of April.

Your calmness, centeredness, and power are now anchored forever within your consciousness. This will begin to nurture all other aspects of your creative desires that will contribute to success on your journeys. Some of the most prevalent characteristics that will be noticed are increased creativity, better judgment, greater ease with words and expression, and more confidence in the powers of manifestation. This position of focusing your thoughts and having greater concentration does not come until approximately sixty days after such an experience. This is the reason why the memory capabilities of each group member have been so affected in the last several weeks.[2] *In order to assimilate all of this new learning, the physical brain structures were altered to allow for the neuron mechanisms to receive the higher vibrations. Since no two things can occupy the same space at the same time, something momentarily has to go. The memory capacity has been altered to allow the memory programming for these higher states of learning to be slowly assimilated into your brain structures.*

We trust that, when you understand this, you will not be as discouraged as we perceive you have been in the past. This condition is only temporary. Know that we would never do harm to you, and that we are actually providing you gifts for wisdom and understanding far beyond what you have previously experienced.

The "story of significance" we have relayed this evening actually carried with it two points of power. The first is that higher consciousness is a gift from the God Force that is both received and earned by the soul in embodiment. Second, all children of Light move on the same path to enlightenment, and it is this path that contains the truths and answers to secrets which free souls to enter Shamballa.

We live in Shamballa, a city you will soon enter on a more permanent basis. "We come from the ethers and journey to the stars" to provide you with the keys and the codes to your destiny. Allow us to continue this dialogue now with our interpretation of what that magical saying means to us.

On the ascended realms, the ethers mean the gaseous intelligence that comprises the prana of the universe. It is that which is the essence of all life and which breathes love and Light into a soul. Its origin is the Great Central Sun, and the form and shape that it can take is directly dependent upon the individual or life form who chooses to breathe its substance into manifestation.

The etheric state of beingness is realized when one's consciousness has been elevated to the Fifth Dimension and higher. This state of awareness is equivalent to the third eye opening and the doorway to the inner planes of enlightenment shining through to one's soul. Realization of the path one needs to travel to achieve enlightenment is the first step to achieving this state of Godhood.

To say we journey from the ethers implies that we have come from the substance of God. It suggests to us that we are of the Divine and that we are and always will be of that life force. The only thing that changes along our path is the shape and form we choose to manifest, both within and outside ourselves.

*On the seventh dimensional frequency, the manifestation powers not only are taken for granted, but also are accelerated to the point that "what we **will**, is what manifests". On the fifth dimensional frequency, the rule changes somewhat, for there are other vibratory patterns that must be considered before manifestation occurs.*

First, the Fifth Dimension is the halfway point between Earth and the ascended realms. Therefore, the physical, manifest world and its curriculum of Light must be integrated with the will and visualization powers that we take for granted. In order to become a fifth dimensional Being, one must look to the Divine on the higher planes and integrate that which is known on the physical plane to form the creation. In so doing, the Fifth Dimension is created within the mind energy of the individual. It is

149

the etheric form of love and life that is breathed into the souls of humans.

*This dimension is powerful, for it is that which comprises the cosmic glue of emotion. Emotion is considered to be the **will** with which you work on the third dimensional frequency. The will for us is different than the will and emotion that you must master. But that is a different lesson for your benefit that could be sent at another time.*

To say we "journey from the ethers and move to the stars" implies we are the shapeshifters and starmakers of the universe, for we combine knowledge of universal law and mastery of the etheric to create stars deemed to be of the highest radiance. Humans are only now learning to do this as they transcend the physical world and access the Fifth Dimension. This is demonstrated through revivals of spiritual paths and in awakenings occurring around the world.

It will not be we who birth the beloved Terra into a star in the universe—it will be you. The blueprint for your perfect part of the plan is contained within your own Higher Selves. This plan is awaiting integration with your consciousness.

In the etheric, the star to which we have journeyed at this time is awaiting your awakening. Earth has been connected to all higher dimensional frequencies from its creation. It is only the consciousness of the souls who inhabit the planet that have not been connected. Therefore, Earth awaits to provide you with the knowledge and wisdom on how to do this. All answers are contained within her essence. Hear her voice and cry in the wind for direction as to how to proceed. All knowledge is contained within her connection to your own Higher Selves. Clear the channels, Oh Dear Ones, and know that the paths for your future will come from direction through the heart centers.

This concludes our interpretation of the phrase, but this is not to impose this interpretation on you or others who will be charged with decoding the meaning in accordance with your own Higher Selves. It is important to say this, for we do not intend to give away any of the secrets to future souls who choose to make this sacred journey to discover the wisdom of the ancients.

This interpretation was provided to inform you that the day has come (when you were in the vortex) that solidified your measurement of how close you are to accessing the blueprints within your Higher Selves. Each of the thirty-four voyagers who traveled to Bimini is on the path to becoming one in the Kingdom of Adam Kadmon, which is the place of the perfect fifth dimensional human being. There is much that must be accomplished before this is realized, but we tell you with confidence that it will come to pass. That vortex and its electromagnetic field serve as an accelerating device for this to occur and provide the means by which souls can travel into the Light in less time.

This concludes one, final interpretation of what actually occurred when you made this sacred journey, but this does not conclude the information needed for understanding the complexity and totality of the mission. For the final information I relinquish the frequency to El Morya, who awaits to provide instruction on the law and how your journey served to alter the destiny of the beloved Terra.

Thank you for this opportunity to serve you in this way. I am honored that you have taken time to request our interpretation. The Tribunal Council looks forward to the next session, when we will again be asked to provide more insight into the blueprint and the cosmic plan that is definitely being created in this parsec of the universe.[3] *Good day, Dear One. I now relinquish the transmission to my Brother in the Light. Adonai.*

[After another pause and energy shift, the following message from El Morya was transmitted.]

Greetings, Bright Star.

I come to you today to deliver my words of gratitude and appreciation for the work that has been completed thus far. You and the other spiritual warriors completed a mission for Earth that is deemed to be of great significance for the work we are doing at this time. The event has shaken the etheric and the reverberations are sounding far into the universes. We speak not of distance in this explanation, but instead of distance transcended by time and space, as you know them to be.

The impact that your journey had for Earth can be stated simply:

> *The doorway was opened for the powers of the seventh dimensional frequency to move freely within the ley lines and grid lines, to touch Earth's electromagnetic power centers with such magnitude that the sound of creation will once again be reborn on the planet.*

The negative energy blockage from the vortex you entered thirty-five miles east of Bimini was so potent that it was causing great disruptions in the work we have been trying to accomplish on Earth. This unilateral obstruction was caused by the condensed Atlantean energies from long ago, and has been building in intensity for thousands of years. Since this vortex is so powerful, it has been a root cause for much negativity on the planet. Much of the pain and sorrow has originated from this source. It is only now that you feel the effects of the released energy you have emancipated.

The law stated that this vortex was to remain untouched for centuries to allow it to "fester", because in the etheric there were many astronomical changes and influences that required time for completion. In this present moment, Jupiter rules with such might that it oversees many disrupting forces which have potential for causing much chaos on the planes and seas. If this vortex had been allowed to generate more negative energies, there was great concern for the planet's survival, knowing that the powers and influence of this great protector, Jupiter, were moving with a force and ease that could result in much upheaval.

If the vortex had been cleansed earlier than your stardate of February 10th, 1991, many of the accomplishments in the physical plane that have been completed might not have come to pass. The other variable that required acknowledgment was that this vortex could only be activated when the seventh and third dimensional frequencies were synchronized in the etheric. This occurs once every twenty-six years. Looking into your future through the hourglass of time, if this vortex had not been neutralized, there was great concern that Jupiter and its effects would cause so much upheaval that there would be little left to admire on the face of the beloved Terra. Therefore, it took the courage and dedication of ones such as yourselves to make this journey, and, therefore, allow others to benefit also.

A second benefit the planet received from your dedication was a programming for the future. The programming was translated from the oldest language known to humanity and received within the fourth dimensional frequency to assist in cleansing the negative psychic strata that surround the planet. What this will now allow for is a rush of the violet frequency to penetrate the structure of Earth. This activity will provide many souls with a higher and more positive outlook on life.

The coding that was received in the Fourth Dimension is available to decode by the masses, if they only turn their thoughts to goodness and Light. The fears and illusions that keep them trapped are only that—traps to lower their vibrational frequencies. Know that your journey and efforts will directly affect all inhabitants of Earth in the years to come, and feel the warmth of their smiles as they treat you with an inner respect they do not understand.

You will walk your paths in higher vibrations; your auras will reflect the tribute you have made to God; your lives will be adjusted according to your new stature. This is assured, for the time of the countdown is upon all. Feel the gratitude and warmth from the masses in the months and years to come, and know that the journey to the sacred place in Bimini is indeed the agent on the physical plane responsible for allowing all of this to happen.

The real journey that you experienced, of course, is that within your minds. Everything that is and always will be is contained within this life force. Know that your journey is not over, but has only begun. See your radiance increase as you continue to decode the messages for your individual paths in the years to come.

Many group members are feeling the power of this life force flowing through their veins and hearts. This anticipated reaction is the result of the breath of life that each experienced when each made the commitment in the vortex on that important day.

For those who made the commitment to become one with their Higher Selves, this life force is now flowing to assure its speedy reunification.

For those who made the commitment for greater clarity and cleansing, their paths will be filled with the toxic waste being left behind. We remind those souls to understand that it is important to bless all that is being released on a regular basis, and feel the love and gratitude that draws them closer to their own Higher Selves. Offer all which is released to the ascended realms and request that the energies be transformed into the highest and purest energies known for use on the planet.

For those who took the journey to become more firmly anchored in the physical plane, we state with much commitment that you will experience the journey in your future in a way that will provide you with all the physical comforts you will need to enjoy your existence in the days and years to come. This is a given, and we are pleased to provide you with such reinforcers. Know that none of you shall want for long, and that pride in your work and lives will be granted, only if your commitment remains first to God and then to the serving of your fellow humans. This is so.

Reach for the stars, Oh Dear Ones, and see the radiance shower you with comfort and Light. The plan is to allow all once again to assimilate their thoughts with the centeredness within their minds, so that all will become one with their missions.

For many it is already becoming apparent that a move of physical distance is inevitable. This is a part of the plan,

*for the journey to Atlantis was only the first step in form-
ing the community of the Highest.*

*When the mind energy of Matreiya and the Most Radiant
One is truly anchored on the beloved Terra, you will then
understand your journey and the significance of your
important work. This is scheduled to be anchored by the
year 2011, and will provide all with the elixir that is
sought to sustain life in your world and ours.*

*This elixir was first discovered in Atlantis, and will be
rediscovered in the years to come by the souls who will
rise again to reclaim their power. The Light within will
radiate so brightly in these destined souls that they will
not know fear, illusion, or the voice of deceit. Instead,
they will feel only the connection to God and their own
inner source of power that has lain dormant for so many
years.*

*The mind and heart connection within one's centered state
of beingness is the key to understanding how to reclaim
power and to drink this elixir of life. This connection is
truly the step toward mastery, but the beliefs that must be
changed to achieve this state are many. Know that the
voice of truth and wisdom is always in one's heart, and
that the intellect teaches discernment to find it.*

*Feel your strength arise, Oh Children of the Divine,
and carry the Light of freedom and truth with you wherever you go. Journey to Atlantis with us in the years to
come and expel the incorrect perception that Atlantis is
lost. Find the souls you were with in that former lifetime
and journey into the unknown to reunite with their essence. When you come to this vortex, come on bended
knee and know only that God awaits to redeem all of the
lost children who wish to reunite with the Light of
creation.*

We direct, protect, and guide all who wish to join us in this dimensional frequency. We send no soul away. This promise is assured to those who make the journey with the heart and mind connections assembled for the inward journey to find their Higher Selves. Fear not, and know that all illusions are only lessons of discernment to allow each to pass tests of initiation with honor and respect.

This concludes the words that I was asked to deliver at this time. On behalf of the Tribunal Council of the Galactic Command, I, El Morya, now close this communication.

We humbly thank each of the guests whom we had the privilege of serving on this journey, and state emphatically that we look forward to guiding the others who will choose to do the same in the future.

Go in peace, love, power, and Light as you walk hand-in-hand with the Divine. Bless all you address in the years to come. Adonai.

---

[1] In the December 26th message, Kuthumi described the three paths that would be established for the group members, following the trip to Bimini. This statement is referring to that message.

[2] In the days and weeks following the trip, many group members kept in contact with one another. In the course of conversations, it quickly became obvious that they all were having difficulty focusing their thoughts and remembering details that they took for granted before journeying to Bimini. Kuthumi was referring to this situation in this part of the message.

[3] This statement apparently refers to additional information the Masters are sending through while this book is

being written. They have requested that another book be completed that describes the universal laws, a part of the hierarchy, and instruction for moving into the Fifth Dimension. At this time, that book is only in the formative stages.

CHAPTER XIX:
MORE MYSTERIES UNVEILED

AFTER THE messages were compiled and the introduction and summary written, Jean and Norma decided
that there were many questions to which a reader might
want answers. The intrigue of the entire experience
opened up one mystery after another. As a result, a list
of pertinent questions was compiled, with input from some
of the group members. This effort produced the following
information, which provides additional interesting reading, especially for those who wish to make the journey in
the future.

All questions in this chapter were answered by Master
Kuthumi. The information came through in many sit-
tings, over a two-month period of time. Although Kuthumi
always opened each transmission with his normal intro-
ductions and greetings, the decision was made to print
only the responses to the questions in this section. The
formal opening statements thus were deleted.

The first session began with an intriguing question
that all group members had asked at one time or another.

WHAT ACTUALLY WAS (IS) BELOW THE OCEAN
THIRTY-FIVE MILES EAST OF BIMINI THAT CRE-
ATED THE VORTEX?

*The center of energy that created the vortex thirty-five
miles east of Bimini was none other than the Atlantean
seat of power. In that vortex, three remembrances still*

159

exist which have caused tumultuous disturbances on the planet.

The first remembrance comes from the human conscious-ness released during that fatal day of the destruction of Atlantis. The fear that was generated not only terrified Earth, but also sent a scream into the heavens heard as far away as Alpha Centauri.

Second, a crystal chamber for the most powerful electri-cal-laser production unit ever developed in Atlantis was situated in the Temple of Heronne in that area. In this temple many of the "finest" minds of the Atlantean civili-zation studied and conducted research, refining their inventions with higher intellectual discoveries.

The inhabitants of the temple built the greatest laboratory and institute of advanced mathematical research known to the world, creating a vortex of scientific knowledge that is unmatched even today. They understood the music of the spheres, and integrated sound frequencies into all their discoveries. This knowledge gave them the keys and codes to ancient mysteries.

The power the crystal chamber created within the Temple of Heronne is still active today. Its effects continue to be felt around the world. It has been a primary cause for many of the negative vibrations that have manifested throughout the planet, for much Atlantean knowledge was used for destructive purposes in the final days. These vibrations constitute the second remembrance found in that vortex.

The last remembrance programmed into the vortex was the primordial scream. This is the blueprint of the begin-ning times, when the third root race fell into the pull of matter and momentarily lost the path and way to the

160

Divine. Today, many descendants of the third roo *and of higher divinities are making their ascensions. ..ʌt the original fall of that fatal day, and the pain the souls endured, were registered in this etheric whirlpool. These are the energies contained in that vortex.*

HOW WILL UNDERSTANDING THE KEYS AND CODES HELP US AND THE PLANET IN THE YEARS TO COME?

Understanding the keys and codes will not help, if integration of the knowledge is not accomplished. That is why we so frequently stress discipline and right use of will. To know something is only one level of the process. To actually "be" that knowledge is to understand how to facilitate its impact.

In years to come, forces of darkness will continue to push souls to the edge of tolerance. You already see this manifesting around you in tragedies that befall beautiful souls who inhabit the world. Many believe they are victims of the tragedies, but we say, with much assurance, that there are no victims, for each draws to himself or herself whatever is his or her focus of attention. Sometimes it is a subconscious focus, or what is stored in the akashic records, that propels reality. That confuses individuals, which is why many do not see the point we are making.

What must be understood is that focusing attention on the Light of the Most Radiant One and the love of the All vanquishes all lower vibrations emitted from an individual's consciousness. It is likened to erasing all karmic debts, and serves as the redeemer for lost souls who wish to see the Light.

The keys and codes you learn to integrate in the days ahead will assure that you are receptacles of the Christ energy which is flowing into your world. It is this energy that will transform and transmute all things. But to be one with this power, one must first be an instrument of its love. Integration of the Christ energy into the cellular structure and mind of the individual assures that only higher thought forms and actions will result from one's consciousness. When in this mode, the power of the energy provides shields for protection from forces of darkness and assures safe passage through the darkest of times.

Many souls understand the importance of love and hear how Light protects one's essence, but fail to believe in or practice its use. Without integration, the Force passes through like water through a funnel, and the protection is lessened when the mind competes for thoughts of both higher and lower natures. The results manifest many different events in one's life, when centeredness and dedication are not present.

This is why integration is the key. When one chooses the path of love and Light, that individual integrates the mind, heart, and physical body in a way that assures safe passage. When one is integrated, knowledge of the keys and codes is given as a gift to allow the person to gain more power for use in service to others.

So, to answer your original question, of how this understanding eventually will help each of you and the planet, is to say that it will transform the beautiful Earth into a radiant star in the heavens, worthy of the return of the Most Radiant One.

IN ORDER FOR US TO COMMAND AN UNDERSTANDING OF THE CONCEPT "CHRYSTHOLEN", WHICH IMPLIES THE LANGUAGE OF THE HIGHEST, HOW MUST WE DISCIPLINE OURSELVES?

The first statement of importance is that chrystholen is not a concept. It is a language of symbolism that has its imprinting in the etheric. The fact that it is contained in the etheric denies it conceptual attributes, for the term "concept" is reserved to things, ideas, and events of the physical, manifest world.

To command an understanding of this highly evolved system requires one to restrain one's mind from using logic and the patterns that are so feverishly programmed into its operation. Understanding this etheric system demands alignment with one's Higher Self to access the etheric coding systems which provide universal, vibrational keys and codes. In addition, one must learn the universal laws, master them, and apply them each moment of the day and night. This vital step supports understanding of chrystholen.

The elders of Atlantis knew how to access levels of awareness and dimensions that only a few are beginning to comprehend today. Those in charge of the laws and governing principles of that lost continent were selected because of their profound abilities to use the chrystholen. They had transcended all earthly knowledge and extended their understanding to higher frequencies of existence. They could peer into the Fifth Dimension by applying laws that transcend Earth. They had access to the future and the past, and could read akashic records, which allowed them to rule from a supreme position.

To command an understanding of this higher body of knowledge requires discipline of mind to use only universal laws and the keys and codes of higher kingdoms. This demands constant dedication to the application of the knowledge, and requires much time. The student on this path learns laws that are far above normal human consciousness patterns. One never comprehends the meaning, the application, or the process if one does not dedicate the time to assimilate knowledge within the heart area. Finally, the final application of truth and the test for mastery rest in the individual's ability to use the power for humanity and not for ego.

IN THE MEDITATION ON BOARD THE BOAT, WITH WHOM DID OUR HIGHER CONSCIOUSNESS CONNECT AND WHAT DIMENSION(S) DID EACH GROUP MEMBER EXPERIENCE?

To answer that question for each group member would require that we give you seventeen different answers. Since that would take too much time, allow us to summarize briefly in the following way.

Each group member experienced individual connections to the hierarchy guiding his or her path. There were seventeen Ascended Masters who guided the thirty-four Starseeds on the journey. Of the seventeen, five of the Masters responded in that vortex to the subjects making the contacts. One Master was assigned to each level of commitment. We will give you the order in which the contacts were made, and the nature of the commitment for each level.

Those souls who connected to the Divine and made a commitment to serve God first, and all else second, were connected with Sananda. They were made aware of the seriousness of their missions and were instructed that the duty and honor needed to make such a commitment would be guided and supported by the highest celestial forces in this part of the universe. They also received confirmation with the Seal of the Seventh Sign, and were made aware that they are committed to serving humanity in helping people find their way back to God. Of the thirty-four, eighteen souls made this contact and received the blessing of the Highest.

A second group of souls made a commitment to serve in the assistants' role rather than in the ranks of leadership. These souls were connected with El Morya for their mission statements. They were instructed on duty, responsibility, and the laws they must follow to be the support team for the Divine. They were told of their glorious futures, and taken to the domain of the Highest for the ceremony and tribute they deserve for their decision. Of the thirty-four, five were honored in this way.

A third group of Starseeds made a commitment to be the healers for the planet. These souls were greeted by Hilarion and were told that their faith would heal the world. They were shown a vision in the etheric whereby the Earth would salute them for their dedication and work in the future. They were blessed by Sananda and the celestial ranks also, and were brought before the Tribunal Council, who conferred their degrees of faith upon them. Of the thirty-four, three were honored in such a fashion.

A fourth group of souls committed to become teachers in the millennium. They were brought before Kuthumi, who guided them in the meditation to the higher realms of knowledge. They were taught the secrets of Atlantis in a private session and were instructed on the plan for education in the years to come. They were given information far beyond their own understanding today, and were programmed with the conceptual treatise that will be revealed through their Higher Selves in the years to come. For their dedication to humanity and to the Command, they were honored and received awards for bravery and enlightenment, for truly this role will be one of the most difficult roles to fulfill in the years to come. Of the thirty-four, five were initiated into the rank of world teachers.

The three remaining Starseeds, who were in the fifth group, communicated with Delphor and were guided to the Temple of Honor for instruction that matched their commitment to dignity and power. These souls committed to become Earth ambassadors for the millennium and brought with them their desire to serve humanity and God in the role of dignitaries. They sought a path to bring peace and harmony to the planet through their own frequencies, and asked for direction on how to fulfill the responsibilities of this path. They were showered with gratitude and love for their choice, and received medals of honor for their devotion and courage in making such a selection.

In the vortex, all Starseeds were connected with the seventh dimensional frequencies and were polarized with the electromagnetic currents running both north and south and above and below. They began experiencing the process of atomic rejuvenation and came five steps closer to receiving the Light bodies within their own electronic circles of power.

WHAT IS "THE SEAL OF THE SEVENTH SIGN" THAT YOU REFER TO IN THE ANSWER JUST GIVEN?

When we use the term "The Seal of the Seventh Sign", we are referring to the divine nature within that is the pituitary gland of the brain structure in humans. The pituitary has the capacity of emitting an elixir that allows the divine energy to flow into one's consciousness, connecting humans with higher states of consciousness and with God. The pituitary, once activated, fills the brain with a distinct electrical frequency that provides individuals with the capacity of sight and wisdom beyond the manifest plane.

SACRED JOURNEY TO ATLANTIS

WHY DID YOU SAY THAT THE INFORMATION YOU IMPARTED IN THE DECEMBER 1, 1990, MESSAGE ON PROTOCOL WOULD BE TAKEN TO THE GREAT LIBRARY CHAMBER AND SEALED FOR SEVEN MONTHS? WE UNDERSTAND THIS ALSO TO MEAN THAT WE CANNOT PUBLISH THIS BOOK UNTIL SEVEN MONTHS AFTER WE RETURN FROM THE VORTEX. PLEASE EXPLAIN.

Allow me first to provide an explanation of the power of the number seven. Contained within this number is the significance of the white Light. Within the Light are the rays of the seven frequencies that provide all creation with life. The number seven is the frequency upon which this universe is created. It therefore contains the vibration and power of strength, love, and the Light.

To seal sound vibrations through words for a period of seven months allows the frequency to move within the universe to all dimensions. It seals the codes contained within the frequency and majestically displays them, at the end of this period, in the beginning of the next octave. This allows the vibrations to permeate the essences of all energies contained within consciousness, and also provides a means by which the vibrations permeate higher octaves as well. This unity bridges higher dimensions and realities with lower ones, consequently strengthening the impact the words have, once they resonate within consciousness.

It can be likened to allowing bread dough to rise for several hours before baking it. Allowing the dough to rest gives it greater flavor, better texture, and a sweeter aroma. Everything is enhanced. Even the weight is lighter.

Sealing vibrations for seven months before placing them within consciousness does the same thing. This action serves to prepare individuals with a higher, lighter frequency that stimulates the pituitary glands within consciousness, which results in a higher, electrifying current penetrating the brain structures.

You are right in your interpretation that it is important to seal the information contained within your manuscript for seven months before revealing it to the public. By following this procedure, you assure a greater impact on the people whom these messages are sent to serve.

DID ALL STARSEEDS ON EARTH RECEIVE THEIR MISSIONS WHEN OUR GROUP WENT INTO THE VORTEX?

If you recall, it was stated in the messages that the ritual and programming each one completed for thirty days before entering the vortex was the actual initiation for your missions. Therefore, because of that experience, it is reasonable to state that only the thirty-four who journeyed into the vortex received programming for their missions. But in actuality this is not the truth. So let us explain.

All children born into the human race come equipped with their divine plan and mission, which is to serve God and to serve humanity. Every soul on Earth has a path and the steps necessary to reach ultimate happiness and glory. This is law and it is truth.

Starseeds have come to Earth with an additional, collective responsibility to dispel negativity and to bring Light into the atomic structure of the beloved Terra. This must be accomplished to fulfill destiny. The New Age is destined to claim a higher frequency, directed by the precession of the equinoxes. Starseeds assist in fulfillment of the mission and transformation, thus assisting the Masters and the hierarchy in the divine plan for the universe.

Programming of the missions for the thirty-four was activated upon entering the vortex. The dates for activation were set when each participated in the activities and efforts completed thirty days before the journey. Depending upon each soul's willingness to serve, and his or her attitude toward responsibility, each was assigned a position of command that matched the commitment to God. This is so. Missions were activated in that vortex and the assignments by the hierarchy are irreversible. At this point, no one can touch the thirty-four individuals—only they can alter their own paths. This can be accomplished through conscious selection or by the lessening of their own vibrational patterns contained within consciousness.

In the future, as new souls travel into this vortex and undergo similar experiences, they too will receive activation for their missions. But keep in mind that this vortex contains energy for souls destined to fulfill only one part of the divine plan. Other souls are now receiving, and will continue to receive, their missions in other ways.

We hope this clarifies your concerns and provides you with additional information regarding your own experiences that day.

YES, THANK YOU. WE WOULD LIKE TO PROCEED TO ANOTHER QUESTION NOW. WERE ALL STAR-SEEDS ON EARTH EXEMPTED FROM FUTURE KARMIC DEBT, OR ONLY THOSE WHO WENT INTO THE VORTEX?

As of your calendar date when Harmonic Convergence converged upon the planet, all Starseeds on Earth were exempted from karmic debts. This is so because the stars were in an alignment of oneness. In that position of alignment, the heavens sent to Earth a violet frequency so powerful that it dissolved debts of all those who were true seekers of Light. This historical event contained the moment of probability where the Masters showered the beloved Terra with much radiance and love. All united forces of the Confederation and Galactic Command were as one in power and commitment to bringing peace and harmony to Earth for the coming decades. Therefore, many Starseeds received telepathic messages through their Higher Selves, requesting that they take journeys to power vortexes on Earth to facilitate higher energies passing through their physical bodies during that period. In other words, they were the conductors for the forces of the Most Radiant One. And because they were gathered in sacred spots, they allowed all energies to be magnified through them around the world.

If you recall, it was shortly after Harmonic Convergence that selected major events occurred on Earth, such as the disassembling of the Berlin Wall. Consciousness changed dramatically, according to our readings, and we are pleased at the accelerated awakening we observe throughout the world.

For the Starseeds who did not feel the planetary shift and cleansing, and who have not realized the absolving of their karmic debts, additional karma has been accrued since that time. We are, however, pleased to report that most of them have stayed relatively free of debt as they have proceeded toward their missions. This is so.

Allow me to clarify one thing before we continue with another question. In reality all individuals on Earth have their ancestry from the stars, since the planet Earth was a colonized area eons ago. Therefore, this information pertains to all who inhabit the Earth. So why, then, do we call only selected individuals Starseeds?

What determines one's "residency" on Earth is how quickly one proceeds through the curriculum. The curriculum on Earth is the understanding of Light and energy and its control through the right use of will, heart, and mind. When souls learn this and live balanced lives in peace, harmony, and oneness with the Creator of the All, they are freed to journey to other places and assume rank on other land masses and stars. Residency in other places is dependent upon both the selection and the invitation processes, for not all star systems allow souls to claim existence. For some, the right to claim residency has to be earned through an understanding of universal laws and an increased vibrational frequency.

Most souls on Earth today are what celestial Beings refer to as Earthlings. This term refers to souls in embodiment on Earth who have not yet learned the curriculum and language of the highest. These souls have had most of their embodiments on Earth only because they cannot escape from the forces that surround the planet which keep them trapped in the illusion of the physical world. When souls embody so frequently in one place because a higher frequency cannot be obtained through an understanding of the curriculum that allows them to leave, they receive their identity from that to which they are attached.

The Starseeds we refer to as representatives of the Galactic Command have not embodied frequently on Earth, because they learned the curriculum of love and Light early in former pageants. They transcended the language and illusion and, consequently, had most of their experiences on stars and in constellations of higher vibrations. Those who match this description, and who have embodied on Earth at this time, know they are there because they volunteered and were selected for assignment. They are among those who follow the teachings of their Higher

Selves and understand the power of love. They intuitively know that to follow the Creator of the All, God, is the only path that will lead them home. And in so doing, they understand that they earn "points", so to speak, for increasing their own vibrational frequencies through service to humanity and handling the most difficult assignments on Earth.

Where this discourse is leading is that, in reality, karmic debts for all on Earth were absolved during Harmonic Convergence. This was the realized strength of the moment. Rebirth was truly recorded in history at that time. We weep to monitor the debts the populace has accrued since that moment.

The law of karma is exact and it is just. Therefore, much has been created that must come to pass in the years to come. If all children of Earth would realize that seeking the Light can change destiny in a moment, all would be realized. But alas, the eyes of the many are blinded by participation in the physical illusion around them.

MANY OF US ARE BECOMING MORE TELEPATHIC SINCE WE HAVE RETURNED FROM BIMINI. IS THERE A CONNECTION BETWEEN THIS OCCURRENCE AND THE JOURNEY WE MADE?

There is a connection, Dear Ones, but it is not only you who are experiencing this. In an earlier communication we explained how your journey opened vortexes worldwide and touched all Starseeds on the planet. This process allowed all to feel and experience the same gifts from the Divine. In experiencing greater telepathic abilities, each is reclaiming the position held in Atlantis, and in this process is beginning to experience the power taken for granted in that lifetime.

SACRED JOURNEY TO ATLANTIS

SEVERAL GROUP MEMBERS SAW UFO'S DURING
THE THREE-DAY EXPERIENCE. WHO WERE THE
BEINGS IN THOSE CRAFTS, WHY DID THEY APPEAR,
AND DID THEY HAVE A ROLE IN WHAT HAPPENED?

*The Beings in the spacecrafts that appeared to several
members guided you on the journey into the vortex. They
represent the legion of Light workers on the etheric who
protect and watch over children of Earth. Some were
from the Pleiades, and others were from constellations
and star systems from other places in the universe, such
as Orion, Lyra, Arcturus, and Venus.*

*Their purpose was to provide a watchful eye over the
group's energy and to guide the direction in which each
was going, in the event that any group member needed
assistance.*

*They appeared for the purpose of providing comfort and
the connection to home for each member who connected
through his or her five senses to their presence. They
provided the map for the journey by assisting, from above,
any soul who wished to raise his or her vibrations through
sound frequency. Another role they completed was to tune
etheric bodies by using the ships' technology. In so doing,
they channelled the energy of the meditations to higher
planes for distribution throughout other dimensions.*

DID THESE BEINGS PLAY A ROLE IN THE VORTEX
WHEN WE WERE ALL GATHERED THERE?

*In reality, no-thing¹ or Being played a role in the vortex
except each group member and his or her own Higher
Self. That experience of the oneness and the reuniting of
the cosmic energies were personal experiences for each
soul and complete in their own uniquen. ss. This connection was facilitated by the Ascended Masters who not only*

guide each of you, but who also guide all souls on the path to God. The Beings in the spacecrafts who protected and guided you were doing so out of respect and dedication to your spiritual paths. They would never interfere in such a mission. Therefore, they only waited and sent the highest form of love and Light they were capable of sending to all of you, for they understood that in so doing they were serving all of humankind.

WHILE WE WERE IN THE VORTEX, TREMENDOUS WINDS, EXPERIENCED SINCE LATE FRIDAY AFTERNOON, SUDDENLY QUIETED. PLEASE EXPLAIN IF THIS WAS SIGNIFICANT, AND, IF SO, WHAT MADE THEM STOP.

The winds that began to intensify late Friday were the result of the vortex that was beginning to open at the midnight hour of your arrival. The winds were expressing the energies passing from the Third Dimension to the Seventh and back to the Third. They were the cries and pain of the centuries being released into the etheric to be reprocessed into higher thought forms.

The winds stopped suddenly when the group entered the vortex because of the collective power of your Higher Selves. You stilled the waters with the power of love and Light, and witnessed the effects in the physical world. Your journey was significant because your collective intention and will brought peace over the vortex as you prayed and meditated from the highest point of power that each understands today.

The significance of this event showed you the power of your own true, higher nature, and was destined to impress upon you the importance of using this force from within to bring even more peace and love to the beloved Terra.

WHAT PURPOSE DID THE DHL BOAT PLAY IN THE
JOURNEY TO AND FROM THE VORTEX? WAS IT
ONLY A COINCIDENCE THAT IT CROSSED OUR PATH
TWICE AND NEARLY HIT OUR BOAT ON THE RE-
TURN TRIP?

*The DHL boat was a reminder to all on the spiritual path
not to take any event for granted. Even when one's life is
running in harmony, it must be noted that events can
come out of nowhere to startle the spiritual warrior.
Remembering this truth will prepare all voyagers for any
and all events that may cross their paths.*

*That DHL carrier was selected by the Command to awaken
and startle the group into a state of consciousness whereby
each would question the significance of its passage and
use skills of discernment not normally tapped. Discernment is the key to strength in the days and years to come,
for all on the spiritual path. Discernment is the key to
understanding one's mission and performing it with brilliance. Without discernment one is left with mediocre
results that resemble the path and products from a world
you are leaving behind.*

*The DHL carrier is synonymous with being an interna-
tional traveller. Note that the group of thirty-four had to
journey out of the United States to assume positions as
international communicators. This graphically depicts
the significance of your journey and touches all life forms
living within the Fifth Dimension, for it is in the Fifth
Dimension that all networks of love and Light are formed.
For the spiritual warriors who made this journey, the
DHL boat represented the journey that each is destined to
make in the years to come. Each will startle the world
with the messages that will be heard internationally by
all. This is so.*

YOUR ANSWER IMPLIES THAT THE EARTH WILL NOT BE DESTROYED IN THE NEAR FUTURE. IS THIS SO?

We see in the etheric darker times approaching before they get brighter. We also see that the world is destined to pull itself through the decade of the nineties and beyond, and move to a position of power never seen before in the heavens. While you do have the power to destroy all in a moment, we do not foresee that this will be the case. Through the work of the children of Light and the Christ energy of the God Force working through all who move to love and Light, we see the blueprint eventually building a civilization known as the Seventh Golden Age on Earth.

Know with all assurances that this new civilization will not tolerate the greedy, hateful, and revengeful. For those who choose paths that replicate such patterns, we honor their choices and prepare a planet that matches those vibrational frequencies. We judge not their behaviors. We only allow them a home deemed more comfortable for their energies. In the cleansing of the nineties and beyond, many of these souls will be swept away, and in this process they will understand how everything in the etheric and within the universal laws is perfect.

WHAT WAS THE CHANGE OR INTENSIFICATION OF ENERGIES WE EXPERIENCED WHEN WE WENT NORTH ON THE ISLAND ON MONDAY IN "SEARCH OF THE GRAIL"?

What all experienced was the love of Mother Earth embracing and thanking each of you for your healing energy. It was nothing more, yet everything in the eyes of the Divine. That which embraced you was the expression of the highest form of yin energy present on the planet.

Its nurturing qualities and strength provided each with the at-one-ment required in that moment of time.

WHAT WAS THE SIGNIFICANCE OF VISITING THE FOUNTAIN OF YOUTH, AND WHY WERE SOME GROUP MEMBERS TOLD TO PUT THE WATER ONLY ON THEIR WRISTS AND THIRD EYE AREAS?

The Fountain of Youth implies the liquid that sustains all life, for in reality, life is unending and always youthful. In the physical world there is a remembrance back to the beginning when all were one with the Creator. This memory drives all souls back to the Light, seeking their source and sustenance of energy.

The place in Bimini designated as the Fountain of Youth was once an area which contained energies that allowed humans to balance the yin and yang energies of their essences. In so doing, these individuals lived long lives. They did not understand the passage of death as you know it today. These souls, of course, were the inhabitants of Atlantis, who understood more about creation and the Creator than any soul in your world.

The souls of Atlantis kept a vigil celebrating the perfection of creation by obeying universal laws and living within the unified force field. They understood the unified force field to be the intelligence that supports all life, and knew that this field was not separate from the human species or anything else created on Earth. In this knowing, they built their civilization to reflect the highest form of tribute to God that they could create.

When their knowledge became too powerful for their egos to handle, they began tampering with the laws of nature and the universe. When they began to believe that they, and not God, were the source of all creation and power, they began creating situations that were not in harmony with "the All". In this reality, they eventually created the destruction of the beautiful civilization they loved.

To them, the Fountain of Youth represented the beginning and end of all life. They learned, in the last days, that they actually had created a new beginning, but one which they had not anticipated. The Fountain of Youth ran dry, for they could not fathom their fate, nor could they see the future any longer through the eyes of the youthful, innocent, or obedient.

The energies that provided them longevity suddenly were stilled in their eyes and hearts. The balance of the power was lost, and the continent ripped the etheric with its cries of pain. To the masses, the ideal, which was represented in the Fountain of Youth, was no longer to be found.

But even though Atlantean souls caused the liquid in the fountain to run dry, Mother Earth had the power to nurture her children in other ways, unforeseen even by them. The Fountain of Youth has been kept alive by the Earth's nurturing, ever since the last days of Atlantis. The waters of that underground outlet preserved the yin energies throughout time by not allowing them to become contaminated. Today, this situation provides a sanctuary for those who journey there to partake of the pure vibrations. It provides a haven for many who wish to become one with the vibration of the feminine strength.

The group members who were instructed to place the liquid on their wrists and third eye areas were advised that to do so would provide greater understanding of inner worlds and dimensions. Those points on the body are strategic areas for receiving etheric messages from the Higher Self. The third eye is the gateway to hidden dimensions and knowledge connected to universal consciousness. By swabbing these points with the water's concentrated feminine energies, the openings are increased, allowing higher consciousness to flow. That is why this suggestion was made.

KUTHUMI, AT THE RISK OF ASKING A QUESTION THAT IS PROBABLY AN OBVIOUS ONE, DID WE FIND THE GRAIL WHEN WE JOURNEYED NORTH ON THE ISLAND?

Yes, Dear Ones, you found the Grail by journeying north on the island. This is always accomplished within the heart area when the feminine energies are reunited within consciousness. To journey physically into an electromagnetic vortex enhances this activity and provides a boost in the reunification charge within. This is true for all such power points on the planet.

For the group of thirty-four, each also found the Grail in another way on another dimension. This is to say that each group member discovered this holy symbol within the heart by the commitment each made to be a spiritual warrior for God. This was truly the significance of this journey for all of you.

DO OTHER STARSEEDS HAVE TO TRAVEL PHYSICALLY TO BIMINI TO RECEIVE WHAT WE DID FROM THIS JOURNEY, OR CAN THEY JUST READ THIS BOOK AND BENEFIT?

The answer to this question lies at the heart of the situation we posed to you on this journey. The answer comes in two parts:

1. *First, the spiritual journey one takes always comes from the heart center through the Higher Self.*

No individual making a spiritual journey in the physical world, who has not made a clear connection to the Higher Self, will ever fully benefit if they have not first made this connection. So, the first part of the answer is that before any individuals can move into the higher dimensions of the etheric, their minds, hearts, and souls must be prepared with "right thinking", "right intent", and "right will". This is accomplished by passing lessons and tests experienced in the physical world.

2. *A second part to this answer is that each individual dedicated to receiving the opportunity to participate in all twelve initiations on the spiritual path MUST, at some time, physically journey to the vortex in Bimini. This could be accomplished in this lifetime, BUT COULD ALSO HAVE BEEN COMPLETED IN A PREVIOUS ONE.*

There are numerous positions for spiritual warriors on Earth today, but those who wish to proceed to the portal of the Fifth Dimension with maximum power and centeredness must confront their greatest fears and guilt. The journey to this portal is now prepared for all who have not formerly made this journey, to make the spiritual trek to face the akashic record memory of their greatest fears and guilt, by facing the final moments of the fall of Atlantis. This is so!

*Many individuals may challenge this instruction and say that it is not accurate, for they understand the power of the etheric movement within, and how Masters command forces from within. We say unto them, that the souls who are preparing for the final journey today are all in **physical** mastery, and a part of the journey requires cleansing and*

*releasing. It is for these souls that we have pre-
pared this portal, for this is the releaser of the negativity that will hold them back if they do not journey
there to face their final moments.*

*Much fear held within is actually that which each
remembers as his or her own participation in the
final cataclysmic days of Atlantis. Each must work
to free the consciousness of the power of the illusion
that keeps them from accomplishing the missions.
By facing this dream and moving energy on the
conscious level, each will be released to receive the
programming for the higher missions of the Divine.
Therefore, we say unto ye again, that this journey is
necessary.*

SINCE OTHER INDIVIDUALS MAY ALSO NEED TO PHYSICALLY TRAVEL TO BIMINI, WILL WE BE NEEDED TO ACT AS GUIDES FOR THEM?

*The answer to this question is both yes and no. Allow us
to discuss the "no" answer first.*

*Starseeds journeying on the same path that each of you is
on demonstrate similar capabilities to those you have
earned. They follow their own inner guidance from their
Higher Selves, for they are in oneness with Light and
centeredness. Therefore, it would be inaccurate for us to
state that they need guidance other than their own inner
direction.*

*However, many Starseeds do find comfort in the fact that
the support of other physical, sentient beings alleviates
moments of frustration and doubt, especially when they
are in the stages of learning to communicate accurately
with the Higher Self energy. In this capacity, the*

assistance of any soul who has already made this journey would be of great benefit.

From our perspective, the individual who assists other souls on this journey of facing their final fears and guilt is truly a sister or brother of Light. The journey for others who will enter this same portal will be just as easy, and difficult, as it was for all of you. The individual who can comfort new group members could be an asset to the future spiritual warriors who will make this journey into the unknown.

Does this answer your question, or do you wish for us to elaborate further?

[Jean and Norma discussed this answer and decided that the information was sufficient for the present moment. They then decided to change the subject and asked the following question.]

FOR THOSE STARSEEDS WHO JOURNEY TO BIMINI, WILL THE AGENDA AND THE MESSAGES BE THE SAME AS THOSE RECEIVED BY OUR GROUP?

The coded information received for your journey is universal. Contained within the messages is the understanding of the mysteries of the ages. The information includes all that the Starseeds need to make the journey into this portal of time/space. There is nothing more contained within or outside of one's consciousness that could provide any more information for the transforming soul journeying into the Light at this time.

To say that this is the only information one needs for mastery is inaccurate, and that would mislead you. We state again that the messages contain all the information needed for this window of time to successfully complete the journey into the Atlantean vortex.

IS THERE A LIMIT ON THE AMOUNT OF TIME THAT INDIVIDUALS HAVE TO MAKE THE JOURNEY?

We have repeatedly stated that, in the etheric, there are no such things as time or space. It is important to begin this discourse with this reminder, for that is critical to understanding our answer to your question. We have stated that the vortex thirty-five miles east of Bimini is an area which transcends time and space. This is so! That is because this vortex supports seventh dimensional frequencies uniting with the lower plane, which affects power points all over the planet by magnifying Light and love vibrations that transcend limited concepts such as time and space. This vortex is one of the few which allows individuals the opportunity to unite with their Higher Selves and journey to higher planes of consciousness.

The journey the thirty-four completed in this vortex opened up a window of space and time for the next millennium. Your physical presence prepared this portal to receive future souls of Light who will journey to this location to remember the divinity within, and to make the sacrifice it will take to move into the unknown.

This experience has no time limits, for the time constraints one might place on this experience would be inappropriate for the purpose of the journey. The time constraints placed on this experience should be those that each individual chooses to place. How long do you wish to wait before you achieve your mastery, Oh Children? How long do you wish to wait before you are one with the Higher Self and the divinity within? In reality, you are already one with this force, but in your separated forms and in the illusion, you do not understand.

One of the reasons consciousness is blocked is because the fears and guilt harbored in your akashic records remain from those last days of Atlantis. The faster one journeys into this vortex, the closer one moves to reclaiming the understanding of the higher dimensions of consciousness that unite you with your own divinity.

Therefore, the only time constraints placed on this journey will be those which are self-imposed.

FOR OTHERS WHO CHOOSE TO MAKE THE JOURNEY, WHAT PROCEDURES SHOULD BE FOLLOWED?

Procedures come in two forms. The first procedure that must be respected is to honor yourself and your own Higher Self. This assures that the use of force and will are contained within the God energy and that ego plays no role in the journey. Therefore, preparing oneself to make the journey by respecting universal laws and practicing discipline and love are the first procedures that one should follow.

The second set of procedures that should be considered are those that assure safe passage into the vortex. Therefore, the messages must be read and studied through the Higher Self, and the information should be processed with the same dedication that we observed in the group of thirty-four. Know that in giving comes receiving. The amount of time one gives to practicing integration of the keys and codes will be matched with the understanding of the mysteries received from one's own akashic records.

Procedures for the trip are simple. We observe that it is discipline in mastering the procedures that is not so simple. Humans on Earth are easily distracted, which means that focusing the will is a challenge. In Atlantis, focusing the will was their greatest talent, which is why their powers were so great. Their challenge was learning to adhere to universal laws and allowing only Light to guide their paths.

We see in the spiritual warriors of today the total dedication to the Light, but we also see the absence of disciplined wills. Not until individuals attune these two qualities will the power and knowledge be regained.

WHAT IS THE NEXT STEP FOR GROUP MEMBERS AFTER THEY RETURN FROM THE JOURNEY?

The coding for this is simple. Wait one calendar year before making major changes in mind-set energy within consciousness. This time period assures that all will be "set" and the formulas will be in place to allow integration of the energies. This position frees the individual to contemplate what is happening to him or her. Trust us when we say that this rest period is needed, for the cleansing and releasing that occurs in the vortex is one of the most profound energy shifts witnessed on Earth.

A second thing that must be done is to keep a schedule for meditating. We cannot stress this enough, for this practice assures the releasing and unlocking of the mysteries contained within the akashic records. After six months of this practice, request to be taken to the Temple of Athena in the Great Central Sun to learn of the wisdom of the Greeks and how they graced the world with incredible knowledge. They were the great ones, along with their sisters and brothers of Egypt, who formed the collective vessel that kept the Atlantean energies alive. Keep the vigil in this temple on a nightly basis and discover the chambers within your own consciousness where all records are kept. Know that the world awaits for each of you to reveal the contents. There are 144,000 parts to this vault, and each spiritual warrior who comprises membership in this group contains one piece of this library in his or her akashic records.

All is contained within the etheric. All souls have access to the information, but only after each soul unlocks the doorway to its contents. Once this is done, the collective consciousness has access to the beauty and wisdom contained within the vault, and the entire world benefits from the process and understanding.

First, teach yourselves the process of love and Light. Then, go inward to release the secrets to share with the world.

IN THE BIBLE THERE ARE REFERENCES TO THE 144,000 INDIVIDUALS WHO STAND BESIDE JESUS. HOW WOULD YOU DEFINE THIS GROUP?

To begin, the number 144,000 adds up to the numerical equivalent of nine. The strength of this number is that it represents the completion of a cycle and the preparation for the new journey that lies ahead. This number is the actual count of the number of souls who will align themselves to the Christ energy in the seventh dimensional frequency. The souls occupying those stations represent the twelve Tribes which were the descendants of the second root race that inhabited the Earth. They are the original caretakers of the Mother and are once again directed by inner vision and wisdom to occupy the roles of the prince and the pauper.

The word "prince" is selected because each soul is truly a descendant of the Lord and is the manifestation of Adam Kadmon, soon to walk the Earth again. The word "pauper" is selected to represent the spiritual poverty each has had to experience in this lifetime, in finding the path back to the Great Central Sun. These souls know not of deceit or evil, for their auras shine like bright stars in the heavens. Presently, they live in all places on the Earth and journey only inward to the higher realms for their sustenance.

There is no selection process for enlisting the dedication and service of these wonderful Light bearers. They select themselves. The laws are becoming clear in their consciousness and they are quickly becoming one with their ascended guides.

Some call these souls "disciples". We choose to call them spiritual Light keepers. Others admire their strength, which they find in love, while still others fear them because of their capacity to love.

In this lifetime, all of these souls will be rejoined in the Father's mansion to celebrate the long tour of duty. Each soul has, in some previous lifetime, taken the position of accepting the Christ energy into their nine bodies, and all have also died because of their belief system. They have come again to be reborn from the womb of feminine energy, and to learn to balance that with the masculine energy. When each soul learns to do this by centering the heart and calming the mind, the nine bodies will again align and all power will be restored. Until that day of perfect balance, they must journey to find themselves through their own inner channels.

IS EVERYONE WHO JOURNEYS TO BIMINI AUTO-MATICALLY ONE OF THE 144,000?

*In the heart and higher consciousness of **each** individual, there is a connection to the 144,000. In reality all on Earth are of this number. The power of being one in membership comes from the completion of the cycle of* *death, whereby the soul had ended the journey of life and also transcended death. Primarily this occurred in the King's Chamber of the Great Pyramid of Egypt. In time, all souls will achieve this mastery. In this lifetime and era we foresee only 144,000 who will complete their journeys.*

Not all who travel to the vortex outside of Bimini will complete their nine-year cycles in preparation for the new beginning. Those who do will rejoice at the gifts and inner calmness it will bring. Those who do not complete their cycles will rejoice at the raised consciousness they will receive that will help them on their paths. There will only be winners. The consequences of not making the journey are nil also, for God's plan is truly to provide perfection for all.

KUTHUMI, YOU HAVE SUGGESTED THAT SOME INDIVIDUALS MIGHT WISH TO PREPARE FOR A SECOND JOURNEY, THIS TIME TO THE HIMALAYAS. IS THE TRIP TO BIMINI CONNECTED TO THIS FUTURE JOURNEY?

The two journeys are connected by a gossamer thread of golden Light that transcends the third dimensional, manifest plane. The two power points we have directed you to need love and Light. They are two of the most powerful places on the planet for the evolutionary progress of humankind. Within these vortexes are the keys and codes that humanity needs to unlock the mysteries of the ages, which will assist all to the Fifth Dimension. Contained within one vortex are a portion of the answers needed to free the minds and hearts of the many. Contained within the other vortex is the other half to the understanding that must be released into the universal consciousness for all souls to access.

These two vortexes are connected by a wave of heat energy that provides a balance for the world. They help stabilize the Earth's magnetic flux and protect it from another fatal imbalance. To journey to both of these points of power also intensifies programmatic influences within human consciousness that stimulate the pituitary influence. By moving in this vortex, and surrendering to the higher consciousness and universal plan, the energies of the Christ Light penetrate the essence. This condition allows for more Light to penetrate the core of Mother Earth which ultimately increases the amount of feminine energies poured into the Earth's electronic structure.

Therefore, the two vortexes and journeys are connected. One is the compliment of the other, although the experiences designed within each vortex are entirely different.

---

[1]The hyphenation of this word was deliberately inserted by Kuthumi. We believe it expresses an expanded meaning of the words "nothing" and "no thing".

EPILOGUE

SOON AFTER our return from Bimini, many of the group members spoke of experiencing a centeredness and calmness not felt before. There appeared to be a quiet power growing within our minds and hearts that translated into an ability to handle circumstances in our lives with a different level of clarity and strength.

When some of the members began discussing this with people outside of the Bimini group, it was discovered that others were beginning to feel this same sensation. Several of us wondered if this was what Kuthumi meant when he said that our presence in that vortex would affect all Starseeds on Earth.

In contemplating the possibility that our experience in the vortex may have had a positive effect on so many others, we have a feeling of warmth and gratitude that we had this opportunity to serve. It is sometimes difficult to believe that our experience had this effect; yet, the Ascended Masters tell us it is so. In accepting this as truth, there comes a greater understanding of the connection and oneness which we all share, and the knowing that a step forward by one is a step forward for all. In this knowing, we salute and give thanks to all Starseeds for each one's contribution to the whole, and to the success of the Ascended Masters' plan to assist Earth in her evolution to the Fifth Dimension.

BIOGRAPHY OF NORMA MILANOVICH

NORMA MILANOVICH is president of a training and development corporation in Albuquerque, New Mexico. She is also an author, instructor, speaker, wife, and mother. Before starting her own company in 1987, she was an assistant professor for thirteen years in the College of Education at the University of New Mexico. During that time she was also the director of the New Mexico Consortium for Research and Development for Occupational Education. Prior to that she was an instructor at the University of Houston for six years, where she earned her master's and doctoral degrees in education.

During her career Norma has served on numerous national and state advisory councils, such as the New Mexico Advisory Council on Vocational-Technical Education, Southwestern Indian Polytechnic Institute's Technical Advisory Board, and Ohio State's National Center Advisory Board for the Development of Performance Based Instructional Materials. Over the past twenty years, she has presented at many international, national, and state conferences and workshops, and has served as a workshop facilitator on hundreds of occasions. She is listed in *Who's Who in the West, Who's Who of Emerging Leaders in America,* and *Outstanding Young Women of America.* Norma has also authored several professional publications relating to education.

In the early 1980s Norma began arranging study tours for educators and business professionals to study education and training in foreign countries. Her efforts took her to Japan, Korea, Hong Kong, Germany, Mexico, New Zealand, and Australia. The knowledge gained from these experiences began to prepare her for the inward journey she was destined to take that took her to England, Greece, Egypt, and Bimini.

Since the fall of 1984, Norma has received communications from Beings who have identified themselves as Celestials and Ascended Masters, and who say they have a message for the people of Earth. The first transmissions she received resulted in the book *We, The Arcturians,* published in 1990. It is through individuals like Norma that these Beings hope to help the people of Earth through the transition into the New Age and into the Fifth Dimension. The communications will continue to be published as guides to help individuals understand what is happening, not only to the planet, but also to each of us as we progress on our own sacred journeys.

SACRED JOURNEY TO ATLANTIS

BIOGRAPHY OF JEAN MELTESEN

JEAN MELTESEN is a native Californian, born in the city of Glendale, just north of Los Angeles. She lived in southern California all her life until moving to New Mexico in 1982.

She attended schools in Glendale and entered California State College at Los Angeles after graduating from high school. After two years of college she married, and within four years had given birth to two sons who are now grown and currently attending college in southern California.

Jean has pursued many different career areas and jobs in her working life, with several related to local and state government, both in California and New Mexico. Jean describes her adult life as "a personal odyssey of inner examination and spiritual growth". A student of metaphysics for fifteen years, Jean was moved by Spirit to relocate with her children to Santa Fe, New Mexico. She spent six and one half years in Santa Fe, and describes that time as one of "intense learning and growth". Circumstances moved her to relocate once again to Albuquerque, New Mexico, and there she began a period of even more accelerated growth.

In August of 1989, she met Norma Milanovich and one month later had a reading from Ascended Master Kuthumi which altered the course of her life. Within a year, she quit the work she was doing and began working on various projects, utilizing her writing and creative abilities. She has now come to understand that her new career path was actually preparing her for greater things to come, leading her to her destiny.

When the trip to Bimini came into view, Jean knew this was an important journey for her to make. As the plans for the trip unfolded, Norma received information from Master Kuthumi that there would be a book written about the trip, and Jean was asked to be the co-author.

Jean feels she is receiving guidance from St. Germain and other great Masters, and attributes her interest in writing to the guidance and instruction she receives from the ascended realms.

As for the future, Jean has been informed that there are other books on the horizon for her to write, if she chooses. Under the guidance of the Masters, she hopes to do so, and fulfill her dream of "assisting others home to the Light".

BIBLIOGRAPHY

Cayce, Edgar. Under the editorship of Hugh Lynn Cayce. *Edgar Cayce on Atlantis.* New York: Warner Books, 1968.

The Holy Bible. Chicago: Good Counsel Publishing Co., Inc., 1965. (Published with the approbation of His Excellency Walter A. Coggin, O.S.B., Ph.D., D.D.)

Carson, David and Sams, Jamie. *Medicine Cards: The Discovery of Power Through the Ways of Animals.* Santa Fe, New Mexico: Bear & Company, 1988.

Webster's Dictionary. New York: Lexicon Publications, Inc. 1989 Edition.

GLOSSARY

ADONAI

Hebrew word for the Lord. A manifestation of higher Light consciousness. The pronouncement of the Holy Name Jehovah (or the name of the God of Israel) to which is attributed the power of working miracles. The revealed absolute Deity, the Holy Creator, the Redeemer. Used consistently in these transmissions by the Masters as the seal or ending to each message.

AKASHIC RECORDS

All that occurs is recorded in the akasha, which is etheric energy vibrating at a frequency that records all of the impressions of life. Each individual can learn to access these records by developing inner sight.

ARCHANGEL MICHAEL

The Angelic Being referred to as the prince of heavenly hosts who is the defender and protector of the faith. He is commander of the celestial army and uses the sword of blue flame to vanquish the forces of darkness. [From Hebrew, "who is like God".]

ASCENDED MASTERS

Those who have mastered time and space and gained mastery of the self, fulfilled their divine plan, and ascended into the presence of God, where, because

of their great love, they receive new direction to
teach in many worlds.

ATLANTEAN HIGH PRIESTS

The elders of Atlantis who understood the ancient
mysteries and universal laws. They held the highest positions in Atlantis. They understood that
divine thought came from the source of all creation, but some became so confident in their own
thoughts and inspirations that they began to think
they were the source of all power. As a result, some
of them made decisions that bypassed the connection back to the Creator, which ultimately
brought disastrous consequences to the planet. Their
knowledge was said to be so elevated that they
actually understood the mysteries of creating a
universe.

ATLANTIS

The lost continent described in the works of Plato,
Francis Bacon, Ignatius Donnelly, Pliny the Elder,
Edgar Cayce, and many others; which held a vast
and highly advanced civilization capable of
interdimensional communication, the ability to control sound and Light, and the ability to transcend
time/space. This civilization was reported to have
been destroyed through the misuse of these powers.
The continent sank as a result of the destruction.
Many scholars agree that the continent of Atlantis
probably occupied much of the area now covered by
the Atlantic Ocean.

BIMINI

Two small islands, approximately fifty miles east of
the Florida coast, which are a part of the Grand
Bahamas, and located within the Bermuda Triangle.
The vortex of Atlantis, which Kuthumi and El Morya

directed this group to visit, is located thirty-five miles east of Bimini.

BLUEPRINT

As used by Ascended Master Kuthumi for this document, the divine plan or mission for each of us which is programmed in our Higher Selves. This plan was activated when each group member entered the vortex.

CHRYSTHOLEN

The golden light that remains in the universe at all times. It implies the language of the Highest and demands the greatest discipline to learn. Only the Ancient of the Ancients who had earned the highest positions in the civilization of Atlantis had learned this scripture and its power.

CODES

The symbolism used by the Tribunal Council of the Galactic Command to deliver the keys that contain the secrets to the power Atlantis once knew.

COMMANDERS

Starseeds working for the Galactic Command to help carry out the plan for assisting planet Earth and her inhabitants in their transition into the Fifth Dimension.

CREATOR OF THE ALL

Another name for God.

DELPHOR

An Ascended Master known as the Diplomat of the Divine and the voice of the Sixth Dimension. The Being who guards the doors of the openings to other dimensions and gives instructions to those who wish to enter on how to do so. He also guides Starseeds home when their missions are completed on Earth.

DIMENSIONS

A system of graduated planes of existence, in which each successive plane expresses a higher vibration. Each dimension is comprised of seven levels of vibrations and has its own unique curriculum.

Third Dimension: The plane of Earth's existence, physical matter, and manifestation, ruled by the five senses. It contains dense matter and adopts the curriculum of the carbon-based existences.

Fourth Dimension: Scientists regard this dimension as time, along with the three spatial dimensions of height, width, and length. The Celestials refer to the Fourth Dimension as the vibration of love and the opening to the heart area. It is an etheric dimension that provides the pathway to the higher worlds.

Fifth Dimension: The dimension beyond time/space that allows for pure thought manifestation. Often it is regarded as the dimension of thought.

Sixth Dimension: A higher etheric world that integrates new colors and sounds into its existence; the doorway to the Seventh Dimension. Certain star systems, such as Alpha Centauri, have evolved to this vibratory frequency and reside in this dimension.

Seventh Dimension: The vibratory frequency that begins after the forty-second octave and continues through the forty-ninth. The etheric frequency that supports the Ascended Masters and Shamballa. It contains one of the highest vibrations in this universe. In the Seventh Dimension, Light and sound manifestation are brought to one of the highest frequencies that humans are able to comprehend.

DIVINE WILL
The will of God.

EL MORYA
An Ascended Master who is reported to be Lord of the Blue Ray. He expresses the attributes of power, authority, and law. Some writings state that he was Solomon in an earlier embodiment. El Morya was the Master in charge of the journey to Bimini.

ETHERIC
The all-pervading essence of creation, filling all space and interpenetrating all matter. The holder of all unseen events. All things exist first as ideas or thought-forms in the etheric before manifestation into the physical.

GALACTIC COMMAND
A fleet of starships comprised of Masters and Celestial Beings from numerous galaxies and ruled by the Ascended Masters of the Great White Brotherhood (White meaning white Light), who are helping Earth enter the Age of Aquarius. They travel the universes and have the capability to influence and direct God's plan for continued evolution. They are highly advanced Beings who do not necessarily appear in a third dimensional form. They have assisted Earth in its evolutionary path since the beginning.

GREAT CENTRAL SUN

The center, or core of white fire from which the spiritual/material universes emanate. (Sirius, the Dog Star, has been the focal point of the Great Central Sun in our section of the universe, but over time this position changes, because of the precession of the equinoxes.)

GREAT LIBRARY CHAMBER

An etheric vault of records located in the Great Central Sun containing all information known by the Ancient of Ancients. Access to these records requires approval by one's Higher Self. Using the library chamber requires that the individual has earned a certain vibrational level to assure that he or she has mastered self-discipline. This stipulation is set to help assure that the individual will use the information with wisdom, once it has been revealed.

HIGHER SELF

The Christ Self, the I AM presence, the exalted form of selfhood.

HILARION

An Ascended Master who is reported to be Lord of the Green Ray. This ray expresses the attributes of healing, constancy, and abundance.

HOLY GRAIL

The vessel that contained the blood of Christ, supposedly brought to England by Joseph of Arimathea. Many knights of King Arthur's court went in search of the Grail. Symbolically, it is the quest for the union with the Christ Self that is within each of us.

KEYS

The clues that unravel the mysteries to the secrets

of the power of Atlantis and, ultimately, the creation of the universe.

KUTHUMI

An Ascended Master known to be the World Teacher, who serves Sananda (Jesus the Christ). References cite Kuthumi's former embodiments as including Pythagoras; St. Francis of Assisi; John the Beloved, the favorite apostle to Jesus; and emperor Shah Jahan, the Master who built the Taj Mahal. In his last embodiment he was known to have the name Koot Humi.

LIGHT BODY

The electromagnetic body existing in the ethers. The "real" body that provides the blueprint for the physical body and allows interdimensional communication.

LORDS OF THE SEVEN RAYS

The Ascended Masters who preside over the seven rays, or the Light emanations of the Godhead which emerge through the prism of Christ consciousness.

MAJOR POWER POINTS

The location of power vortexes on the Earth's power grid.

MOST RADIANT ONE

The Ascended Master who is said to be Jesus, the Christ, or Sananda. The Supreme Commander of the Celestials who oversee Earth's transition into the millennium.

ORION COUNCIL

The council which regulates the laws administered in this part of the universe. This is the highest governing body for this quadrant of the universe and is subject to no laws of its own, except obedience to the Great Divine Director. This council regulates many different star systems and planets. The Karmic Council that governs Earth, and regulates the incoming and outgoing lifeforms from the Earth through Arcturus and the Bootes constellation, is only one division of this governing body.

PORTAL
A doorway, entrance, or gate on Earth that leads to higher dimensions; e.g., the vortex thirty-five miles east of Bimini, over Atlantis, said to be a portal to the Seventh Dimension.

SANANDA
Jesus, The Christ, also known as The Most Radiant One.

SHAMBALLA
The etheric city over the Gobi Desert which is the home of the Ascended Masters.

STARSEEDS
Souls from other planets, star systems, or universes, who answered a call for assistance, and agreed to come to Earth to help with the healing and transformation of this planet. Individuals in embodiment who are presently working with the Ascended Masters and the Galactic Command to help fulfill the divine plan of bringing peace, harmony, and love to Earth.

TERRA
Another name for Earth, sometimes used to describe Earth after it has completed its transformation into a star.

THIRD EYE

The "psychic" eye located in the middle of the fore-head and between the eyebrows. Also the location of the sixth chakra. A connection to spiritual energy that can be activated by meditation and awareness. Produces second sight or extrasensory perception. The inner eye of God.

VORTEX

A whirling mass of spiraling energy. Earth has a grid of power vortexes which receive and put out energy.

YIN AND YANG

The broad or universal expression of female (yin) and male (yang) energies. The yin expression is creative thought, and is receptive, nurturing, and intuitive. The yang expression is outer-directed, seeking, and questing, and is the action that carries out creation.

IN APPRECIATION...

LEE SMITH, presently of Chicago, decided to visit Bimini in 1980 to see the sites Edgar Cayce had referred to regarding "The Rising of Atlantis". He was so impressed with the island and the feelings he experienced there that he made a commitment to come back on a more permanent basis.

The goal for his return was to set up a facility to assist others to view the stones of Atlantis, the Fountain of Youth, and the Lithium well, as well as to facilitate other quests they might have. Lee is the proprietor of a small resort with three cottages housing up to fourteen guests. He encourages visitors to come to this special place to practice holistic medicine and to use alternative healing methods.

It is because of the unsolicited help he gave our group that we wish to thank him by including the following information in our book. Lee can be reached at either of the two addresses listed below if you, the reader, want further information about Bimini:

4141 N. Kenmore   P.O. Box 611
Chicago, Il 60613   Bimini, Bahamas
(312) 528-8251   (809) 347-2483

WE, THE ARCTURIANS

The first volume in **ATHENA PUBLISHING'S** New Age Series, *WE, THE ARCTURIANS* was written by Dr. Norma Milanovich, Betty Rice and Cynthia Ploski and appeared in August 1990.

The book is a selected compilation of messages transmitted through Dr. Milanovich via microcomputer from Beings who identify themselves as Celestials from the star Arcturus and members of the Galactic Command. These transmissions describe, in detail, their home, Starship, mode of functioning, way of life, their mission, and Earth's transition into the New Age.

One of the more unique features of this book is that the Arcturians state they are preparing the way for the return of Jesus, the Christ, whom they call Sananda.

To obtain a copy of *WE, THE ARCTURIANS*, fill out and mail the coupon below.

For several years, Dr. Norma Milanovich has received numerous messages from Beings who identify themselves as Ascended Masters and Celestials from the Galactic Command. So much interest has been generated by these transmissions that she found it impossible to reply to inquiries about them on a personal basis. Therefore, certain messages of special interest to the general public are selected and published periodically in the quarterly newsletter, *Celestial Voices.*

The first six newsletters cover a significant six-step process for guiding the people of Earth into the Fifth Dimension. These transmissions are received from Master Kuthumi.

To order your subscription of *Celestial Voices,* fill out and mail the coupon below.

CELESTIAL VOICES

Please enter my name for a subscription to *Celestial Voices* Newsletter. Subscription rates (check your choice):

☐ 1 Year @ $12.00   ☐ 2 Years @ $22.00

Price outside the U.S and Canada: $18.00 per year

Name _____

Address _____

City _____ State _____ Zip _____

☐ [MasterCard] ☐ [VISA] (check one)

#_____ _____ _____ _____ Exp. Date:___ ___

Signature _____

Send check or money order to
ATHENA PUBLISHING
Mossman Center, Suite 206, 7410 Montgomery Blvd. NE,
Albuquerque, NM 87109-1574   FAX (505)880-1623

THE TEMPLAR
IN THE SEVENTH GOLDEN AGE

The Trinity Foundation, organized in 1991 to implement the Templar project, presents a videotape entitled "The Templar in the Seventh Golden Age". This tape documents the speech given about the Templar project by Dr. Norma Milanovich, author of *We, The Arcturians,* to the United Nations Parapsychology Society on October 3, 1991.

For information and updates on the Templar project, call:

1-900-988-0023, ext. 557

The cost is $2.00 per minute with a 2 minute minimum. A touchtone phone is required, and persons under 18 must have their parents' permission to make this call.

— — — — — — — — — — — — — — — — — — —

Please send me _____ copies of the videotape **"The Templar in the Seventh Golden Age"**, at $29.95 each, plus $5.00 for postage and handling. (New Mexico residents add $1.72 per tape state sales tax.)

Please send me _____ copies of Master Kuthumi's message to the United Nations Parapsychology Society, at $2.00 each, plus $1.00 for postage and handling. (New Mexico residents add $0.12 per copy state sales tax.)

☐ I wish to be placed on a mailing list to receive further information about the Templar Project.

Name_____

Address_____

City _____ State _____ Zip _____

☐ [MasterCard] ☐ [VISA] (check one)

#_____ Exp. Date:_____

Signature _____

Send check or money order to
ATHENA PUBLISHING
Mossman Center, Suite 206, 7410 Montgomery Blvd. NE,
Albuquerque, NM 87109-1574 FAX (505)880-1623

NOTES

NOTES